# A BAKER'S YEAR

# A BAKER'S YEAR

Twelve Months of Baking
and Living the Simple Life
at the Smoke Signals Bakery

## TARA JENSEN

 ST. MARTIN'S GRIFFIN  NEW YORK

www.stmartins.com

Designed by Steven Seighman
Photographs by Tara Jensen

The Library of Congress Cataloging-in-Publication Data is available upon request.

ISBN 978-1-250-12738-9 (paper over board)
ISBN 978-1-250-12739-6 (ebook)

Our books may be purchased in bulk for promotional, educational, or business use. Please contact your local bookseller or the Macmillan Corporate and Premium Sales Department at 1-800-221-7945, extension 5442, or by email at MacmillanSpecialMarkets@macmillan.com.

First Edition: February 2018

10  9  8  7  6  5  4  3  2  1

*To my mom and dad, who taught me to be kind and work hard in equal measures, and to my brothers, who were always lighting things on fire*

# CONTENTS

www.followthesparrow.tumblr.com

DEAR FRIEND,

Baking is a technique by which heat is gradually transferred from the surface to the center, changing a raw foodstuff into something edible. This process straddles the line between science and superstition. Choices we make concerning a bread or cake have as much to do with chemical reactions as with how we woke up. Starting from scratch, one must understand and abide by the specifics. Once the basics are mastered, it becomes clear there are NO RULES.

The draw of a wood-fired oven is in the quality of heat. It immediately affects anything in its presence. Penetrating to the core in a short period of time evokes an internal lightness and an outer ruggedness. This mountain bakery, Smoke Signals, is an oven in its own right. Here, pressure and circumstance have cooked me from the inside out.

I arrived at this humble homestead many times. Initially, I came as a seeker: searching for a baker and his bread. Now, years later, in a series of twists, I am responsible for upholding the cycles of flour, culture, and fire.

The greatest lesson I have learned is the value of commitment. While parts of my life imploded, lighting a fire gave me something to wake up to. I have heard it said you don't marry the perfect person; you marry the person you're with when you're ready. I found myself here, desiring a union, so I wed an old oven.

This choice has left me outside of a culture of immediate gratification. It takes several days to bring the bread and oven together in harmony.

Yet I am not immune to the pervasive effects. We have lost the ability to communicate face-to-face, preferring instead the company of a touch screen. We fall in love with impressions. Most bread today is exactly that: an impression. Filler, not food, has become the normal.

I beg you to build a circle of wonder around your baking and protect it. It is a small act that contains the greatest effort: to remain awake, to remain adaptable, and to remain in love. Don't toss it aside. Don't trade it in. Stay and practice. Your kitchen is a laboratory of the sacred order. Time and temperature will find you in the correct place.

As we make bread, we make ourselves.

Warmly,

tara

JANVARY

I raise my hand as your witness.
— posted january 16

The bakery wakes in spring, peaks in summer, winds down in fall, and sleeps in winter. The deepest part of the coldest month is suited for reflection. A time when the experiments of last year are evaluated, celebrated, and laid to rest. The silence draws out a nostalgia. I have come to this place several times, as many iterations of myself. Personalities layered like a stack cake. Although I traveled the country baking professionally through my twenties, baking has evolved into my own personal practice. The rituals and rhythms of flour, water, and fire allow me to process a changing world. This little strip of land has watched me become a woman.

What I refer to as the bakery is two buildings, one my home, and the other, a one-room kitchen with an outdoor Alan Scott oven and tiny upstairs apartment. The space was transformed by Jen Lapidus into a bakery in the late nineties under the name Natural Bridge; my role here is to steward a timeless mission once printed on Jen's bread bags: TRUTH, LOVE, AND GOOD BREAD. At some point it will be passed to the next wayward baker. I am but a housekeeper sandwiched between a historical reenactment and the future in which economic systems have collapsed and we are returned to our own two hands. I make the most of my time. And occasionally watch it slip through my fingers.

When I first passed through the door, Jen was already absent. Dave Bauer, hailing from Wisconsin, had reclaimed the space under the name Farm & Sparrow and was making what was rumored to be the world's best bread; I sought him out. Borrowing a car, I drove the thirty minutes from Asheville to Madison County: the jewel of the Blue Ridge. I got lost, of course. Finding a row of men sitting in front of a bar that was also a general store that was also a tea shop, I inquired for directions. They called the bakery by various names—it was indeed familiar. One had done the electrical. Another remembered building the oven. The most I gathered was *keep going*.

Drive through the junkyard past the rafting company. Take a left between the fire station and the hairdresser. At the end of the tobacco field, take a right. Go past the abandoned gas station. If you reach the river, you've gone too far. Watch out for the dogs that chase cars and the rooster in the road. Take a left at the teal mailbox.

People weren't lying. The bread was good. Some of the best I'd ever tasted. Naturally leavened. Starters made with 100 percent whole-grain flour. Wet, loose dough. Hand shaped. Long fermentations. Blazing hot oven. It was my first glimpse of how breads and ovens evolved together: a

whole working ecosystem of flavor. I left the next day to
take a baking job on the West Coast, carrying a loaf of
seeded bread onto the plane and consuming it feverishly.

I came back. This time to work at Farm & Sparrow
creating pasties and granola and bagging the holy grail
of bread. I eventually followed Dave when he relocated,
and the little one-room shop went dormant. In the passing
of time, I struck out on my own, learning how to farm
and selling bread and tarts at the local market, illegally
baking out of a barn in an oven that stood on wobbly

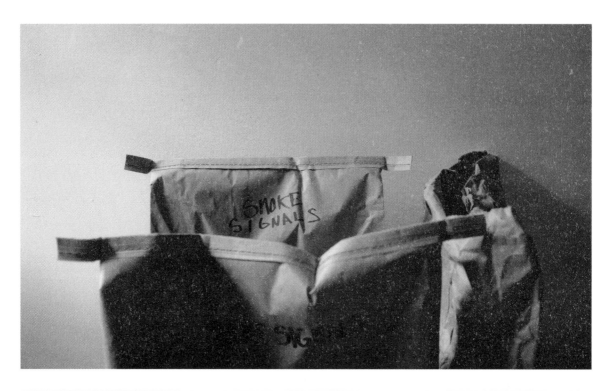

4

cinder blocks. By then Jen had started running her mill, Carolina Ground. When I met her there to pick up flour, she suggested I consider leasing the space, and we came out to the vacant bakery to discuss its future. It needed to be cleaned and resurrected, but it had potential. I scrubbed it on my hands and knees. Washing away my own traces.

The last time I arrived was an internal entrance in the spring of 2015. I was baking pies, and my longtime lover walked out. For good. I went to the door, opened it, straightened my apron, and busied myself with the painstakingly slow process of healing.

There is an undeniable magic here. It must pour from the watering can dangling amidst weathered branches. Or maybe it emanates from the fallen barn behind the roses. Dusty pieces of wands and toys lace the yard. When the cement floor around the oven was poured, Jen and her daughter pushed in tiny mirrors and gemstones. Visitors bend over to try to pick them up. This place is like that: a shiny penny in rough bramble, hard to extract.

Above the workspace, the guest rooms smell like summer camp. I go there in the cold to lie down and inhale. It calms me. I watch my breath curl in the frigid air. The smell is my friend. The way the light falls is my friend. The milk truck. The bags of grain. The rocking chair. The polyester quilt. The woodpile. The dying pond. The picnic tables. These are my companions.

Everyone who has lived here left an imprint. Scratches on the door: tattoos of a dog asking to be let out. Lines on the wall: a child marking height. Stray piles of bricks: a mason taking lunch. Bleached-out floor: the shadow of where a mill once stood. My addition is a wooden triangle at the end of the drive, along with four deep grooves in the living room floor under my writer's chair.

Nothing has taught me how to bake more than simply living here. Positioned in the center of a swirling wheel, I mark my hours by chopping wood, feeding cultures, and making fires. Although I am alone here, I am not the only living thing. The starters bubble and gurgle with temperamental yeast, and the flames crack and boom against the fire brick. Each loaf pulled from the hearth is a record of sunlight, stone, and sentiment.

When the temperatures drop, my main responsibility is to keep the pipes warm. The landscape here is jarring. Tight passages mean portions of the road never see the sun. I think twice about leaving. The pantry becomes important. Pickles. Coffee. Flour. Sugar. Nuts. Popcorn. Spices. Vinegars. Oils. A few bottles of wine. Bags of onions. A sack of garlic. A basket of squash. And, of course, jars of grain.

## ABOUT GRAIN

Wheat is no more wheat than an apple is an apple. Every variety has a particular texture, flavor, and aroma. Variations expand based on growing practices, milling styles, and preferences in preparation. Get to know the nuances of each variety. It will change everything about how you bake. Like making a friend, what was once ill-defined and unknown becomes unique and special.

Modern wheats fall into roughly three categories:

### Hard or soft.

Hard grains are higher in protein and suitable for bread making due to their ability to trap gas and hold it over a long period of time. Soft grains are lower in protein and best for pastry or dough where a weaker gluten structure allows gases to pass through. The bran of hard wheat is brittle, and when stone milled, cracks into the flour, making it difficult to remove entirely and creating a radiant golden-brown flower. The bran of soft wheat is tender, coming off in large swaths between the millstones. Larger portions of bran lead to easier extraction culminating in a light, creamy-toned flour.

### Red or white.

Red wheats have a deep rosy hue and tannins in the bran building a robust, peppery, and occasionally bitter taste in whole wheat goods. White wheats have a fawn or straw-colored bran, achieving a sweeter, milder flavor even with 100 percent of the bran present. Red wheats are higher in protein—perfect for naturally fermented, chewy, hearth breads—while white wheats, lower in protein, shine in crispy crackers, toothy noodles, and lush pan loaves.

### Winter or spring.

In regions with mild winter temperatures, wheats are planted in the fall before Thanksgiving and harvested at the onset of summer. In bitterly cold climates, spring wheats are planted after the last frost and processed in the fall. In general, spring wheats have higher levels of protein and a more elastic quality.

As a basic grass, wheat is designed to nourish itself, protect itself, and reproduce. The germ, endosperm, and bran each play a role in this unfolding mission. In seed form, wheat has been a vital storage crop to many cultures, crossing oceans and continents in pockets and jars. However, once crushed into flour, it should be used as fresh as possible to honor the flavor and aroma.

The smallest portion of the berry, the germ, is packed with fats and fragrant oils. The embryonic heart, it is from here the taproot sprouts and growth begins. The endosperm makes up the majority of the overall berry, a starchy and protein heavy storehouse providing long-term nutrition as the grass grows. Residing in the endosperm are two important proteins: gliadin and glutenin. When hydrated, these proteins lock together in a web-like structure called *gluten*. Gliadin is responsible for the extensibility in a dough, while glutenin imparts elasticity. The bran, the visible outer coating of the berry, is a shield against the wilds.

## TYPES OF GRAINS AND CEREAL CROPS

**Einkorn, emmer, and spelt.**

These wheats compose the trinity of grains that fall under the umbrella farro. Known to be aromatic and oily, as well as nutrient rich, these sister grains store amazing flavor, yet structurally the gluten is fragile and viscous.

Einkorn is the oldest cultivated wheat and the parent to many varieties. Found in the tombs of ancient Egypt, einkorn is a taut, flat, fawn-colored grain. Milled, einkorn flour is incredibly creamy and supple. Fragrant and fluid, einkorn flour is sticky when hydrated and quick to ferment.

Emmer is the second oldest cultivated wheat. A medium-size ruby-beige grain with flavors running from a vanilla bean sweetness to a mouthful of starchy potato. Although firm, it's tender enough to sink your tooth into. Milled, emmer flour is slightly coarse and smells pleasantly like a barn. Emmer is commonly used in pasta.

Spelt is the largest of the farros. Chew it raw for a milky, honey taste. Whole-grain spelt doughs ferment well and have a taffy-like quality. Hildegard von Bingen, a twelfth-century German nun, claimed that eating whole spelt would not leave the body emotionally drained due to its intense nutritional qualities.

**Kamut.**

Also known as *Khorasan* wheat, kamut is large and golden, with a buttery bite. Milled, kamut has a gritty texture and looks like sunshine ground into a bowl. At once crispy and chewy, it is incredibly high in protein and works well in both pastry and bread, imparting a toasted corn sweetness.

### Buckwheat.

The seed of a tall, slender plant related to rhubarb and sorrel, buckwheat contains no gluten. High levels of starch and oil make an incredibly silky flour that can stand alone in pancakes and crepes. Intensely nutty, buckwheat often finds a good home in pastry.

### Barley.

This straw-colored, round berry has an earthy, mineral flavor. Eaten worldwide in soups, porridges, and teas, barley has a spongy texture and absorbs liquids well. Unlike other grains where the fiber is mostly present in the bran, the fiber in barley is pervasive through the entire grain. Roasted, it is extremely sweet.

### Rye.

This blue-green grain grows favorably in cool climates. Not technically a wheat, rye possesses a vegetable gum that mimics gluten and is responsible for the slick nature of unbaked rye bread. Dense rye breads can taste grassy and dank and have a cakelike crumb. Fluffy and almost purple, rye flour can be used in sweet and savory goods.

### Corn.

While fresh corn is considered a vegetable, the dried seed is classified as a grain. Corn is high in vitamins, minerals, and fiber. Known for its intense color, the red, large-kerneled Bloody Butcher is a bakery favorite, while standard popcorn is a staple in my kitchen cupboard.

# PANTRY PORRIDGE

Makes a robust breakfast and lunch for one or a simple breakfast for two

Each summer my father brings me blueberries from my great-aunt's farm in South Carolina. I freeze a gallon just for January. Begin the night before.

*The night before:* preheat the oven to 200 degrees.

Spread the blueberries on the sheet pan; set them in the refrigerator to thaw.

In the bowl, whisk together the milk, spices, and salt.

Pour the mixture into the pot.

Add the barley and spelt.

Cover.

Bake for 8 hours.

*In the morning:* fold in the blueberries with the wooden spoon.

Top with sorghum syrup and bee pollen.

Eat warm.

### INGREDIENTS

1 cup frozen blueberries

3 cups whole milk

1 teaspoon vanilla

¼ teaspoon cinnamon

¼ teaspoon ground ginger

¼ teaspoon salt

½ cup whole barley

½ cup whole spelt

Sorghum syrup

Bee pollen

### TOOLS YOU'LL NEED

Measuring cups and spoons

9-by-10-inch sheet pan

Small mixing bowl

Whisk

4-quart cast-iron pot with a lid

Large wooden spoon

# FARINA

Makes a robust breakfast and lunch for one or a simple breakfast for two

Farina is a comforting cereal on an icy morning. I make mine from the "mids" at Carolina Ground: a by-product of the milling process that is neither completely flour nor completely bran. It's as instant as it gets.

Whisk the farina, cream, water, butter, cinnamon, and salt together in the saucepan.

Bring the mixture to a boil.

Reduce the heat to low.

Stir constantly.

Cook for 6 to 8 minutes, or until the farina is smooth and creamy.

Top it with maple syrup and a few pats of butter.

Eat hot.

## INGREDIENTS

1 cup farina or "mids"

1 cup heavy cream

2 cups water

2 tablespoons unsalted butter

1 teaspoon cinnamon

¼ teaspoon salt

Maple syrup

Extra butter

## TOOLS YOU'LL NEED

Measuring cups and spoons

Whisk

Saucepan

# POPCORN

Makes enough to fill a 5-quart bowl.

I have a beloved pot dedicated just to popcorn. Leave out the turmeric for a classic version. Adjust the various seasonings to your preference.

Pour in the oil and drop three popcorn kernels into the bottom of the pot.

Cover.

Set the pot on a burner turned to high.

Listen for the kernels to pop.

While waiting, melt the butter in a small saucepan.

Once all three kernels have popped, add the rest of the popcorn.

Cover tightly and shake.

Return the pot to the burner.

Keep it on high heat till the rapid popping of the popcorn dies down.

Immediately pour half the popcorn into the bowl.

Dust it with the spices and yeast and drizzle on the melted butter.

Pour in the remaining popcorn.

Toss together.

Eat right away by the handfuls.

## INGREDIENTS

½ cup vegetable oil

1 cup popcorn

4 tablespoons (½ stick) butter

1 tablespoon turmeric

1 teaspoon sea salt

1 teaspoon black pepper

Nutritional yeast to taste

## TOOLS YOU'LL NEED

Measuring cups and spoons

4-quart pot with a lid

Small saucepan

Potholders

Large bowl

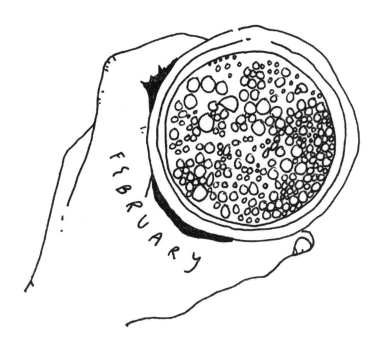

FEBRUARY

Here's how it's going to work.
I jump and then you jump, too.
—posted february 24

I drive through sheets of sleet in search of butter, noticing
beat-up trucks parked in the mud next to greenhouses:
the farmers are milling about. Inside the plastic and steel
wombs, soil is mixed together, flats are filled, and cells are
poked with callused fingers. In goes the barely visible black
speck of an onion seed. Each tray is topped off with more soil,
watered and set on a warming mat. Onions mature according
to day length. Certain varieties take five months to bulb,
requiring they be first on the list of spring seeding. Known
for a pungent sweetness, alliums are traditionally rumored
to stimulate desire. A quality sorely needed in February.

Although the ground lies barren, there is a stirring underfoot. Marginally better weather means townsfolk start socializing again, gathering in the evenings next to a neighbor's roaring woodstove to discuss our plans for the year. It was on such a night I met Camille. I saw her from afar while piling comfort food onto my potluck plate. Her gray hair was twisted into an unruly bun accented by thick glasses, behind which two inquisitive blue eyes peered out. As I lowered myself into a chair next to her, she turned and smiled. Learning that I lived at "Jen's place," she grabbed my biceps and in a thick French accent said, "I like you. You must know how to work."

We spent the rest of the evening discussing the trials and humors of being a single woman in the country. Though separated by generations, our experiences weren't dissimilar. Using a husky, authoritative voice on the phone so the hardware store would take our questions seriously or getting irate when we'd hire a gentleman to work on the house or property and we'd have to justify our visions, providing reasons that would never have been questioned man-to-man. How many times did we have to explain that we understood what a load-bearing weight is! Camille had recently called a store for a roofing quote. They asked if she wanted a lifetime warranty: it was good for twenty years. "How is that even possible?" she asked me. We laughed at the insanity.

Camille came to Madison County in 1972 with her husband, Dave. Dave's father had grown up here, moving to Detroit at the age of nineteen for a better life. He couldn't believe Camille and Dave wanted to return to what he remembered as a desolate region with nothing to offer. They were warned not to come, but their minds were set on it. Enraged by the Vietnam war, they wanted to be as self-sufficient as possible and learn directly from those who could still teach the way of the land. Less income meant minor tax payments, resulting in fewer dollars toward war machine. They took on cows, chickens, rabbits, sheep, and a garden. "A farm is a big name for what we had," she says.

What was big was their ambition. It had to be. It was up against a lot. War was a symptom of an entire broken social system fueled by overconsumption. Refusal of business as usual was crucial to Camille. "I know we have to live," she pointed out, "but we don't need to do it at this level—we don't need to destroy."

Camille had already experienced the horrors of war. In 1944, her childhood home in Normandy was bombed, and although everyone was safe, the devastation left only a corner of the original house. Her family first took refuge in a nearby graveyard, surviving only on milk. There her father decided they would take the two-day walk to his parents' farm, where he was certain food could be found. In the summer, they returned home to rebuild.

Normal weekly rituals ensued, one of which was a trip into town for bread. One afternoon, her sister returned with more than a sack of loaves; she also bore toys she'd found scattered on the roadside. Thin metal rods, like long pens, with a coil wrapped around the middle. They played with them for days, knocking them on rocks like drumsticks. But they weren't toys. They were cast-aside detonators, and while her mother was busy with the wash, one exploded in Camille's hand, causing the loss of her right arm at the age of two.

A decade into their life of resistance, Dave was diagnosed with multiple sclerosis. The long list of daily chores became difficult to maneuver. The cow jumped the fence. The sheep ran away. The dog chased the chickens into the woods. They allowed their responsibilities to dwindle, eventually eating the cow. "It was part of the economy," Camille explained, a firmness still in her tone. Despite changes in physical comfort and energy, they were as true to their original intentions as they possibly could be.

After Dave passed, Camille carried on the design of their home and land, every nook and cranny meticulously thought out and crafted. Stairwells fashioned after the golden spiral, massive mosaic projects, wood scraps and windows everywhere: ideals for a gentle society radiate from the walls. "I never had a course in building," she said, "just an interest. I would look at an old building, I would see that it was still standing, and I would think, *That is good.*" Although Dave is gone, his presence remains, amidst a host of new and radical projects.

Never short on determination, Camille hired a carpenter to frame a door into a dirt wall so that she might dig herself a basement. Rigging up a bucket, a shovel, and a wheelbarrow, she chipped at the top of the wall, directing the dirt downward into the bucket. When the bucket was full, she'd take it to the wheelbarrow and empty it. When the wheelbarrow was full, she'd haul it outside and dump it in the gully. She kept at the work for days and months until rumors began to surface.

Her apprentice who frequented the local bar came to report back on the widespread speculation about what exactly Camille was up to. "You'll never believe what they're saying about you, Camille. They say you are digging out your basement single-handedly with a spoon!"

She chuckled. "Well then, let them think just that."

I spoke with Camille recently. We wondered if it was even possible for future generations to go back to the land. There is increasingly less land to go back to, and the old-timers who knew the plants and the ballads are passing each year. Besides, living the rural life isn't for everyone. It seems that each spring a new crop of young homesteaders arrive bursting with ideas, and only some of them make it to the next year for one reason or another. Many leave when they have children, and divorce is common under the stress of poverty. I like living here because it is so unchanged, and yet sometimes I forget there is a world past the blown-out streetlight. This landscape is a jungle that does not bend to human will easily. Some like the challenge. Some don't.

Yet what we lack in finery we make up for in freedom. We have a choice. We can choose the detonator or the spoon. What will you leave behind? What will your legacy be? Free, gentle, and diverse is the culture I want for myself, my community, and my bread. Be an instrument for peace. Choose the spoon.

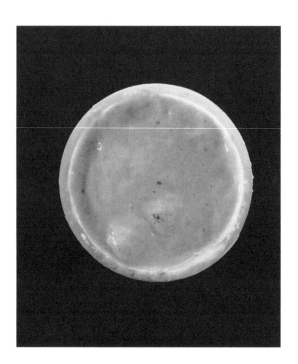

## START A CULTURE

Starting a culture is simple. Maintaining it is the most difficult part. Once established and refreshed, a culture can live for a lifetime, maybe even several. If forgotten, it will not immediately perish or do you harm if ingested. The value of tending a culture lies in the care it needs to stay alive. While we strive to do our best, it should also be a process free of stress.

Standard yeast has one goal: to produce lots of gas relatively fast. Leavening with only commercial yeast cuts out beneficial multiflora from the fermentation process. While a naturally leavened culture takes more time, it unlocks a world of taste, souring the flour and bringing the full flavor body forward.

When water and flour combine, enzymatic activity breaks down starches into sugars. Yeasts metabolize the sugars, producing carbon dioxide and alcohol. This gas is the primary source of leavening in cultured goods. Bacteria, namely lactobacilli, create lactic and acetic acids and very little carbon dioxide or alcohol. A culture is simply the thick batter of flour and water that these yeasts and bacteria call home.

Stone-ground, sifted bread flour from a hard red winter wheat is appropriate to begin your starter with. If it's unavailable, blend whole-wheat flour and bread flour in equal portions. Cultures fed only with whole grain will ferment quickly and can become acidic. Cultures fed with only bread flour, while strong, will taste flat. In any case, remember that this culture is the cornerstone of your future bread. Be consistent in your care, and it will be predictable in its leavening.

# (A) CULTURE (OF RESISTANCE)

Makes approximately 256 grams of active culture

Nutty, loose, and quick to ferment. Look for sweet and grassy flavors to develop over time.

### INGREDIENTS

50/50 whole wheat and bread/flour blend

57 grams whole wheat

57 grams bread flour

113 grams lukewarm water

### TOOLS YOU'LL NEED

Digital scale

16-ounce Ball jar and lid

Spoon

*Day one.* Pick a time that will be easy for you to return to over the course of several days. Use the scale to weigh 114 grams of flour into the jar. Use the scale to weigh 114 grams of lukewarm water into the jar. Stir vigorously. Loosely cover with the lid. Let the mixture rest in a well-ventilated room between 70 and 75 degrees, out of direct sunlight. In general, the kitchen counter is a fine place to begin. Taste it. It will taste wheaty, paste-like, and even chalky at first.

*Day two.* Check back at roughly the same time. Remove the lid and stir well. Taste. Are flavors developing? What does it look like? Smell like? Any signs of life? Replace the lid. Let rest.

*Day three.* Repeat day two.

*Day four.* Early signs of fermentation, such as bubbles and a slight acidic smell, will start to appear. Regardless of what you see, it is time to begin refreshment feedings. Trust that activity has been put into motion. Your role is to keep the movement going. Refreshing around the same time daily will train your culture to predictably ferment.

*To refresh:* Pour out all but 28 grams from the jar and feed it back 11 grams lukewarm water and 4 ounces bread/flour blend. Discarding a high level of culture maintains a low acidity, encouraging a stable environment for the bacteria. It also provides ample food for tired yeast. Several hours after refreshing, check for visible surface tension, a domed top, and dish-soap-size bubbles. In warm temperatures, a bubbly mass reaching the top of the jar will occur within 4 to 5 hours.

At the peak of activity, the culture will float. Test this by wetting your fingers and scooping some off the top and dropping it into a glass of water. Try not to degas the culture as you transfer it. If it sinks, repeat the test in thirty minutes. When it floats, it's ready to use.

Eventually a divot will form on the surface and the culture will begin to collapse in on itself, receding down the walls of the jar. The visible bubbles will turn tiny and frothy, and it will smell quite sour. As this happens, the yeast die off and acidic flavors take hold. The culture is now less active. If you miss the peak, simply refresh it again and let it sit until it passes the float test.

Within seven to ten days from the start date, and with at least three to four refreshments, you should have a bubbling culture that smells sweet and slightly tangy. There are no hard-and-fast rules for how long it will take your culture to come to life. Activity depends on the weather, your environment, what kind of flour you feed it, and how often you check it. I recommend keeping a journal near your culture so you can record when you fed it, what flour you fed it with, the room temp, the weather, and how long it took to pass the float test. This way you have lived experience against the suggestions laid out here.

If you bake infrequently, store the culture in refrigeration. When it has been left dormant this way for a while, allow for several days of refreshing before you plan on baking. I've left mine for up to two months in the back of the fridge at 40 degrees and had it return to life easily. A thin layer of alcohol will form on the top of the culture. This does not mean it has expired. Stir in the alcohol, or pour it off if you prefer, and begin refreshing.

MARCH

LET YOUR SORROW BE GRIST
FOR THE MILL.
—posted march 15

The man who taught me the most about love was also
the man who left me. We met selling bread and
vegetables at the farmers' market. The market would
hold theme days, and I noticed him on Wild West Wednesday.
Usually in cutoffs and a dirt-smeared shirt, he stepped out
in a crisp, blue button-down. He overheard I was having a
bad day and strolled by with a bouquet from the stand he
managed. It was common to trade between vendors, so I asked
him if he wanted a croissant. "No," he said, "they're just for
you." The sound of his voice was a hot knife through butter.

In the beginning of our courtship, I was living downtown, still working for Farm & Sparrow, and he was an hour away, tending crops on a small family farm. On nights when he'd stay over, we'd wake up before sunrise and make pancakes. In those sleepy hours, while the stars speckled the sky, a hot griddle was an intimate gesture. After the season came to an end, he found a cabin with workable land and his own spot in the market. I wanted to farm and test my commitment to baking, so I left my job and started Smoke Signals. We shacked up in the countryside, seeking our fortune.

A parting gift from my baking comrades came in the shape of a beaten tote filled with fifty pounds of Turkey wheat. We spread it on an intensely sloped, freshly tilled field using an old broadcaster the day before Thanksgiving. We had read up on ancient rituals said to increase crop germination. The most common one involved a more figurate "sowing of the seed." So we consummated the act behind the tractor, drunk on a bottle of mead. It sprouted tiny green hairs and then went dormant. We worried about it every day through the winter. It shot up in the spring as predicted, but so too did the weeds and the workload of running a farm and baking. It grew, but not like the amber waves of grain I had imagined. More like a patchy, pubescent beard. When it came time to harvest, we had nearly forgotten our once revelatory grass.

On July 3, with a dull scythe and my grandmother's sewing scissors, we harvested it, standing in the blaring heat, making ragged shocks, and cutting stray heads into pails. We'd let it go a month longer than desired, and I wasn't sure how viable or healthy the grain was. I left the meager yield in a cattle stall near the washstand and carried on.

Weeks later, I returned and filled a pink pillowcase with the wheat heads, beating them with a rolling pin to separate the protective chaff from the berry. Using a ladder, a box fan, and a bucket, we winnowed the wheat. My farmer climbed to the top of the ladder and poured the threshed grain past the fan, the chaff blew in the wind away, and the berries clanked into the bucket below. Each sweet drop of seed against plastic sounded to me like voices in a church choir echoing off marble walls. And yet I looked down at a year of work. I looked up at him. Sweat pouring down our faces mixed with sunburn and dirt. I can still hear myself saying, *There's barely enough for pancakes.*

What happened is more complicated than I am going to tell you here, but the script is classic. Like paint peeling off a barn, our relationship came undone in the years we spent farming. With little to no outside income, we supported ourselves from what we could grow, and the bread barely paid for itself. To say the financial situation was a strain on our intimacy would be an understatement. I baked very little, saving up for weeks on end to purchase a decent sack of flour. Moving frequently to escape demanding landlords or hikes in rent, we lacked stability, and our bond eroded while our hearts grew as callused as our hands. The food around us grew tall and beautiful while the very middle rotted.

I heard rumors before I saw it with my own eyes. On a cool Sunday evening in the early spring, I walked into the local bar and found them sharing a basket of french fries. The way they leaned into each other made my stomach turn. I knew, from that exact second on, that he was going to leave. She was a longtime friend of mine, reeling from a breakup, so I invited her to supper at the house that evening. She declined. He said he had more work to do, so I shouldn't wait up. I ate dinner alone to the sound of a train in the distance. It went on like this. He'd swing by the bar where she worked at night, and I'd eat solo at a table set for two. Eventually I put myself to bed, waking to the sound of his tires on the gravel hours later. The glow of his headlights on the bedroom wall and the sound of the doorknob turning became the opening bars to every country song.

It was impossible for me to leave the house without hearing passing comments on their budding friendship. Getting stopped in the toilet paper aisle of the grocery store to reassure folks that everything was fine became normal. Finally, her boss pulled me aside while I was getting coffee and mentioned seeing them together at her house at a time she knew I wasn't aware of. I walked outside, called him, and told him it was over. We met on the front porch minutes later, and he asked how I was going to survive. I found something I never knew I had: a lucid calm stronger than steel. I turned to him with narrowed eye: "I don't know," I said. "But if I don't respect myself, I'm poor in a way no silver or gold can repair."

The day after he moved out, while I was at the one traffic light in town, they swaggered from the bar through the crosswalk in front of my car and piled into his truck. I pulled over three times on the five-minute drive home because my hands were shaking so badly I couldn't steer. I took the ring he had given me months earlier for our anniversary and threw it into the pond. Starting a small fire in the fire pit, I lay down in the moist earth, and it held me as I cried myself to sleep. My only wish was that I wouldn't have to wake up. Our farmland was miles away from the house, and I never set foot in the fields again.

My psychology was shattered. I'd lost my partner and my way of life. I wondered how cavernous the heart could be that you might lie down beside a person day after day and never know them. Never know how brutal they might turn, or what exactly they yearned for when their eyes shut. And I was embarrassed. In the same bar that we had walked into, arms full of bread and flowers, the languid eyes of our community had watched him fall in love with someone else. I couldn't make eye contact. My pride was the only thing I had, and now even that was threadbare.

The dynamics of a breakup in a small town are particular. With less than 850 people, it was unreasonable to expect that anyone would really chime in on the matter. After all, the majority of the community was older and had already gone through several waves of marriages, divorces, affairs, and other questionable arrangements. So I retreated. Like an elimination diet, I stripped my contact down to a handful of friends and family. I was looking through the eye of a needle, and to pass through, there were things I would have to leave behind. When people conjure a picture of a simple life, they often do not imagine that the primary thing you first must forgo is other people.

I kept the jar of Turkey wheat on a bookshelf in the bakery. The grain was nearly five years old. I liked to check on it every now and then. Like a potion, swirls of perfume radiated from the berries. A cinnamon stick. A dash of pepper. Hay and sweat. Warm soil. It reminded me of what being innocent was like.

A year after he left, I ordered myself a gift. It arrived on a warm afternoon, just before the bread dough was to be divided. Inside a heavy brown box resided a small, tabletop mill. I knew what had to be done. I grabbed the jar, turned the mill on, and let the turning stones transform my most sacred possession into dust. With a slight tilt, years were crushed. Crushed into a fragrant mess. Crushed into something more useful than regret. Turning off the mill, clutching my blue bowl of flour, I leaned into the door frame and wept. Closure is something you give to yourself.

## PANCAKES

A note on freshly milled flour. Stone-ground flour is made by crushing grain between two stones. Milling slowly at cool temperatures ensures that all the original parts of the wheat berry, including the germ, are still present in the final flour. I call this intact, meaning that nothing is stripped away or added back during a later part of the process. Stone milling preserves the fats and aromas that tell our senses we are eating something good for both body and spirit.

Even when sifted, stone-ground flour will have tiny flecks of bran and be coarser than roller-milled flour. The presence of bran and a larger overall surface area result in a flour that can be "thirsty." While freshly milled flour may tolerate high hydrations, it's much easier to add water and adjust to the correct consistency rather than start too high, so that you have to recalculate an entire formula. Go slow, get into trouble slow: start with the appropriate amount of water and then add more as necessary.

# SOURDOUGH PANCAKES

Makes about 8 pancakes

These pancakes are spongy in the center and crispy on the edges. Tangy and supple, they are a household standard at any hour. They call for a bit of sourdough starter. Be sure to bring the eggs and buttermilk to room temp prior to starting.

In a medium bowl, sift together the flour, sugar, baking powder, and salt. Set it aside.

In a separate medium bowl, pour in the active starter.

Add the buttermilk and whisk.

Add the vegetable oil, whisk again.

Separate the eggs into the small bowls.

Whisk the yolks into the wet mix.

Whip the egg whites into stiff peaks with the hand blender.

Pour half of the wet mix into the dry ingredients.

Fold together gently.

Pour the remaining wet mix into the dry and fold just till combined. Do not beat the mixture into a smooth batter; lumps are okay.

Fold the egg whites into the batter in thirds.

Grease and heat a skillet over medium-high heat.

Pour ⅓ cup for each pancake onto the hot and ready greased skillet.

Flip when bubbles rise and pop over half of the pancake, about 2 minutes.

Finish cooking for another 2 minutes or until they are crispy on the edges and golden brown.

Regrease the skillet as needed.

Serve hot.

## INGREDIENTS

**DRY**

1 cup freshly milled soft red wheat

1 tablespoon unrefined sugar

1 teaspoon baking powder

¼ teaspoon salt

**WET**

1 cup active culture (pages 24–25)

1 cup buttermilk, room temperature

3 tablespoons vegetable oil

2 eggs, room temperature

## TOOLS YOU'LL NEED

Small mill or access to freshly milled flour

Measuring cups and spoons

2 medium-size bowls

Flour sifter

Whisk

2 small bowls

Hand blender

Spatula

Butter or bacon fat for the skillet

Skillet

# BLOODY BUTCHER PANCAKES

Makes about 8 pancakes

With a blend of corn, rye, and buckwheat, these pancakes are crepe-like and hearty. The structure of the starter keeps them together, while the grains lend a nutty, sweet, and earthy flavor.

In a medium bowl, sift the cornmeal, rye, and buckwheat flours with the sugar, baking powder, and salt. Set the bowl aside.

In a separate medium bowl, pour in the active starter.

Add the buttermilk and whisk.

Add the vegetable oil, whisk again.

Separate the eggs into the small bowls.

Whisk the yolks into the wet mix.

Whip the egg whites into stiff peaks with the hand blender.

Pour half of the wet mix into the dry ingredients.

Fold together gently.

Pour the remaining wet mix into the dry and fold just till combined. Do not beat the mixture into a smooth batter; lumps are okay.

Fold the egg whites into the batter in thirds.

Grease and heat a skillet over medium-high heat.

Pour ⅓ cup for each pancake onto the hot and ready greased skillet.

Flip when bubbles rise and pop over half of the pancake, about 2 minutes.

Finish cooking for another 2 minutes or until the pancakes are crispy on the edges and golden brown.

Regrease the skillet as needed.

Serve hot.

### INGREDIENTS

**DRY**

⅓ cup freshly milled, sifted Bloody Butcher cornmeal

⅓ cup freshly milled, sifted rye flour

⅓ cup freshly milled, sifted buckwheat flour

2 tablespoons sugar

1 teaspoon baking powder

¼ teaspoon salt

**WET**

1 cup active culture (pages 24–25)

1 cup buttermilk, room temperature

3 tablespoons vegetable oil

2 eggs, room temperature

### TOOLS YOU'LL NEED

Small mill or access to freshly milled flour

Measuring cups and spoons

2 medium-size bowls

Flour sifter

Whisk

2 small bowls

Hand blender

Spatula

Butter or bacon fat for the skillet

Skillet

# BUCKWHEAT PANCAKES

Makes about 8 pancakes

The silky quality of buckwheat stands up against the acidity in the sourdough starter, making a firm and versatile pancake.

In a medium bowl, sift together the flour, sugar, baking powder, and salt. Set the bowl aside.

In a separate medium bowl, pour in the active starter.

Add the buttermilk and whisk.

Add the vegetable oil, whisk again.

Separate the eggs into the small bowls.

Whisk the yolks into the wet mix.

Whip the egg whites into stiff peaks with the blender or whisk.

Pour half of the wet mix into the dry ingredients.

Fold together gently.

Pour the remaining wet mix into the dry and fold just till combined. Do not beat the mixture into a smooth batter; lumps are okay.

Fold the egg whites into the batter in thirds.

Grease and heat a skillet over medium-high heat.

Pour 1/3 cup for each pancake onto the hot and ready greased skillet.

Flip when bubbles rise and pop over half of the pancake, about 2 minutes.

Finish cooking for another 2 minutes or until the pancakes are crispy on the edges and golden brown in the center.

Regrease the skillet as needed.

Serve hot.

## INGREDIENTS

### DRY

1 cup freshly milled buckwheat flour

2 tablespoons sugar

1 teaspoon baking powder

1/4 teaspoon salt

### WET

1 cup active culture (pages 24–25)

1 cup buttermilk, room temperature

3 tablespoons vegetable oil

2 eggs, room temperature

## TOOLS YOU'LL NEED

Small mill or access to freshly milled flour

Measuring cups and spoons

2 medium-size bowls

Flour sifter

Whisk

2 small bowls

Hand blender

Spatula

Butter or bacon fat for the skillet

Skillet

# LEMON POPPY SEED PANCAKES

Makes about 8 pancakes

No starter required in these bright almond-flavored treats: they make the cake in pancake obvious. Serve with citrus jams, powdered sugar, and/or whipped cream.

In a medium bowl, sift together the flours, sugar, baking powder, and salt. Stir in the poppy seeds. Set the bowl aside.

In a separate medium bowl, whisk together the buttermilk, vegetable oil, almond extract, and lemon zest.

Separate the eggs into the small bowls.

Whip the whites into stiff peaks with a hand blender.

Whisk the yolks into the wet mix.

Pour half of the wet mix into the dry ingredients.

Fold together gently.

Pour the remaining wet mix into the dry and fold just till combined. Do not beat the mixture into a smooth batter; lumps are okay.

Fold the egg whites into the batter in thirds.

Grease and heat the skillet over medium-high heat.

Pour ⅓ cup for each pancake onto the hot and ready greased skillet.

Wait to flip till bubbles rise and pop over half of the pancake, about 2 minutes.

Finish cooking for another 2 minutes or until the pancakes are crispy on the edges and golden brown in the center.

Regrease the skillet as needed.

Serve hot.

## INGREDIENTS

### DRY

½ cup freshly milled semolina flour

½ cup freshly milled pastry flour (low protein)

2 tablespoons sugar

2 teaspoons baking powder

¼ teaspoon salt

1 tablespoon poppy seeds

### WET

1 cup buttermilk, room temperature

3 tablespoons vegetable oil

¼ teaspoon almond extract

Zest of 1 lemon

2 eggs, room temperature

## TOOLS YOU'LL NEED

Small mill or access to freshly milled flour

Measuring cups and spoons

2 medium-size bowls

Flour sifter

Whisk

2 small bowls

Hand blender

Spatula

Butter or bacon fat for the skillet

Skillet

# SAVORY PANCAKES

Makes about 8 pancakes

A dose of spices makes these a worthy candidate for dinner. As they come off the skillet, brush with honey and balsamic vinegar. Dust with salt and pepper. Serve with pickled onions, capers, and cheese. Pile the filling in the middle of the pancake, fold, and eat.

In a medium bowl, sift together the flour, baking powder, salt, and coriander. Whisk in the sage and black pepper.

Add the buttermilk and whisk.

Add the vegetable oil; whisk again.

Separate the eggs into the small bowls.

Whip the whites into stiff peaks with the blender or whisk.

Whisk the yolks into the wet mix.

Pour half of the wet mix into the dry ingredients.

Fold together gently.

Pour the remaining wet mix into the dry and fold just till combined. Do not beat the mixture into a smooth batter; lumps are okay.

Fold the egg whites into the batter in thirds.

Grease and heat the skillet over medium-high heat.

Pour 1/3 cup for each pancake onto the hot and ready skillet.

Wait to flip till bubbles rise and pop over half of the pancake, about 2 minutes.

Finish cooking for another 2 minutes or until the pancakes are crispy on the edges and golden brown in the center.

Regrease the skillet as needed.

Serve hot.

## INGREDIENTS

**DRY**

1 cup freshly milled pastry flour (low protein)

2 teaspoons baking powder

¼ teaspoon salt

¼ teaspoon coriander

2 tablespoons fresh sage, chopped

¼ teaspoon black pepper

**WET**

1 cup buttermilk, room temperature

2 tablespoons vegetable oil

2 eggs, room temperature

honey

balsamic vinegar

## TOOLS YOU'LL NEED

Small mill or access to freshly milled flour

Measuring cups and spoons

2 medium-size bowls

Flour sifter

Whisk

2 small bowls

Spatula

Hand blender

Butter or bacon fat for the skillet

Skillet

Pastry brush

# SAUTÉED APPLE TOPPING

Makes about 2 cups

I like buckwheat pancakes topped with the first flush of peppery fall apples, but storage apples are also a real gift through the winter and spring. Goldrushes are my favorite, but Granny Smiths will work just fine. Although this treat goes well on buckwheat pancakes, it's a great addition to any of the pancakes in this chapter.

Melt the butter in the skillet while thinly slicing the apples.

Toss the slices into the hot skillet.

Cook till they are tender and lightly charred.

Stir frequently with the wooden spoon.

Pour in the bourbon and honey.

Let simmer.

Turn off the heat.

Dust with salt and pepper.

Serve piled atop pancakes.

**INGREDIENTS**

4 tablespoons unsalted butter

2 Goldrush or Granny Smith apples

2 tablespoons bourbon

⅓ cup honey

Salt and black pepper to taste

**TOOLS YOU'LL NEED**

Skillet

Knife

Cutting board

Wooden spoon

Measuring cups and spoons

APRIL

I have felt the burn of betrayal and the burn of true love. In the end they are the same burn.
— posted April 11

The belt on the old washer choked out comical groans, filling the house with something other than my sobs. When my grandmother passed away, my grandfather told me he would clap his hands just to hear a sound. I now knew what he meant. I was living in the loudest silence. I began building fires in the oven, even when I wasn't preparing it for baking. It was my way of sending out signals to whatever angels and ancestors might be watching. One morning I glanced up, peering through the multiple windows in the house and through the bakery to look directly into the oven chamber, catching the distant glow of a flame. I knew I had to bake my way out.

I clung to routine as I elevated my bread making from a side gig to my primary source of income. On a stretch of butcher block paper, I wrote the days of the week, and underneath each day I listed the theme and specific duties. Monday: office work. Tuesday: bread mix and oven firing. Wednesday: baking and delivery. Thursday: yard chores and chopping wood. Friday: set up for workshops. Weekend: teaching. Wake up at 5 A.M. Respond to e-mails. No work past 6 P.M. Drink water. Take walks. I taped the sheet to a barren living room wall—it fluttered and echoed in the empty house.

Spring arrived, violent after the starkness of winter. Watercress, dandelions, and chickweed popped up along the creek. Daffodils sprouted and bobbed their yellow heads under the poplar trees. Violets covered the lawn in a tie dye of purple and white. I planted a modest garden mostly of herbs, with the addition of kale, collards, and chard. Snow melted and turned into puddles. Puddles grew tadpoles. The patch of nettles stood tall and foreboding, and rushes of heat in the afternoon warned of summer. Inside the house, there was still a fire at night to take off the chill. The apple trees budded; their vibrant pink blossoms teeming with bees were almost obscene. Everywhere, the crust of winter was splitting open.

On a scarred round of oak, surrounded by sawdust, the start of an 800-degree fire begins. The chopping block is a liminal zone, both a state of mind and an actual place, without which entire rhythms here would cease. Splitting wood, you're neither here nor there. The focus it demands is simultaneously relaxed and poised. You step up to it. You step into it. A basic level of respect must exist between the axe, you, and the wood.

Find a chopping block suitable to your height. Position a log on the block. Step back and look at where you want the blade to land. Lift the axe in both hands, one near the head, the other toward the end of the handle. Hoist over your shoulder so the blade is facing out and the handle is in the air parallel to your ear. The hand near the blade guides the axe. The hand at the bottom is a hinge point. Lower your center of gravity and push off into the swing, pulling the tail of the handle toward your waist and driving the blade into the point you are focused on, allowing your guiding hand to slide down the length of the handle as you swing. To properly split a log, you must look through it.

Gathered from several sources, the wood for the oven isn't split, just the kindling. First, there are Mike and Ruth Anne, who run a nearby sawmill. They deliver pine and poplar skins by the dump-truck load. Mike worked in a bakery as a kid filling cream horns. He always asks if I make them. "No," I always reply. "Good," he huffs. He hated that job. Then there are scraps of hardwood from a furniture shop in Athens, Georgia. Tom delivers it in the back of his white truck when he comes to Asheville. We have tea and catch up on life. The wood is kiln dried and light as a feather, splintering if you look at it hard enough. Last, Toby, who lives down the way, brings a mix of seasoned cordwood. I reserve a portion for feeding the oven in the middle of the night. His off-kilter sense of humor is legendary. One day, while tossing logs from his pickup, I told him I had a rash on my arm that made me nervous. He said I might be dying. I thought I was.

I load crosshatched slabs of sawmill wood into a warm oven after a bake cycle is through. A log cabin arrangement of hardwood kindling is constructed two feet into the chamber, touching the drying slabs. Filled with crumpled newspaper, the lay fire is lit, catching the wood immediately behind it. This point of contact is critical. In time the fire spreads, creating a wall of flame. If the chamber is left open, it takes six hours for the fire to burn from the front to the back. Over time, blue flames replace the bright yellow ones and the gases in the air ignite and slither like red northern lights. The fire is conversational. Hissing, popping, bursting. And then quiet, almost ghostly, nothing more than crispy, metallic tings.

Along with the kind of wood used, the rate of oxygen delivered to the fire determines burn time, temperature, and heat quality. On each side of the oven mouth rest four fire bricks left over from the building of the hearth. Fire bricks are porous, expanding and contracting in fluctuating temperatures without cracking. Once the initial fire has been set and is steadily roaring, the bricks are placed in the doorway, leaving a space in the middle like a gap tooth. Slowing the fire down in the evening leaves a good chance for sleep, although I'm always half awake on bake nights.

To the left of the oven is a covered wood bay. The driest wood lives here and is accessible from the side and the back. In front of the wood bay, attached to weathered posts and beams, is a scrap of plywood that makes up a prep table. Above the oven lives a sheet pan lined with rags I use for steaming while baking bread. A chimney sweep. A long metal rake. A peel and a mop make up the rest of the tools scattered around. Overseeing the makeshift bread chapel is a porcelain Dutch girl, a bundle of lavender covered in soot, and a rusty horseshoe hopefully pointed in the direction that brings good luck.

On the posts framing the oven various trinkets hang. Cast-iron pans. Pruners. A mobile with only two bells in the shape of a crescent moon. A metal spoon so covered in mold it blends in with the smoke-blackened wood. Horsehair brushes with singed bristles for sweeping away debris. A pot where a salty, stiff pair of gardening gloves rests. And the waffle irons. Because I wasn't going to eat pancakes anymore.

## TO START THE FIRE

Campfire waffle irons work best on a thriving coal base.
Prepare the waffle batter while the fire gets going. Heat the
iron on a portion of hot coals. Open the skillet and drop in
a pat of butter. If it sizzles and bubbles, you're in the right
temperature zone. Make sure the area you are building
your fire in is free of flammables and a safe distance from
any structures. Use a shovel to even out the ground.

Gather tinder, kindling, and fuel. Tinder: pencil-sized sticks.
Kindling: branches as thick as the thumb. Fuel: wood the
circumference of your wrist. A few handfuls of tinder, an armload
of kindling, and a knee-high stack of fuel will provide enough
wood for a nice long morning or evening of waffle making.
Although once the fire is established, it can burn wet wood, the
tinder, and kindling you start out with must be completely dry.

Lay two pieces of kindling parallel to each other. Place five
to six sheets of loosely crumpled newspaper between them.
On top of this base, stack ample tinder and a few pieces of
kindling in a Lincoln Logs structure. Ignite the newspaper.
Once the wood has caught, replenish with kindling as
needed. Load on fuel when it's active and burning well.

When done with the fire, use the shovel to break apart
any burning bits and coals. Spread out the ashes, pat
them down, and pour a pail of water over the pit.

# KAMUT WAFFLES

Makes about 8 waffles

The natural sweetness of kamut sings in waffles. The coarseness of the flour makes a cornmeal-like crispy edge with a butter-flavored center.

Ready the coals (page 47).

In a medium bowl, sift together the flours, sugar, and salt. Set the bowl aside.

In a separate medium bowl, whisk together the milk and vegetable oil.

Separate the eggs into the small bowls.

Add the yolks to the wet mix and whisk together.

Whip the whites into soft peaks with the whisk.

Pour the wet mix into the dry mix.

Gently combine.

Fold the egg whites into the batter in thirds.

Grease and heat the waffle iron.

Pour 1 cup of batter onto the hot and ready iron.

Cook for 3 minutes on each side or until the waffle is golden brown and lightly charred.

Regrease the iron as needed.

Eat hot, covered in butter and maple syrup.

INGREDIENTS

**DRY**

¼ cup pastry flour (low protein)

¾ cup kamut flour

2 tablespoons sugar

¼ teaspoon salt

**WET**

1 cup whole milk, room temperature

3 tablespoons vegetable oil

2 eggs, room temperature

Butter

Maple syrup

TOOLS YOU'LL NEED

Measuring cups and spoons

2 medium-size bowls

Whisk

2 small bowls

Large wooden spoon

Butter or grease for the waffle iron

Campfire waffle iron

# EINKORN WAFFLES

Makes about 8 waffles

Waves of cinnamon, sugary sweetness, and a light vanilla flavor make this waffle a favorite.

Ready the coals (page 47).

In a medium bowl, sift together the flours, sugar, and salt. Set the bowl aside.

In a separate medium bowl, whisk together the milk and the vegetable oil.

Separate the eggs into the small bowls.

Add the yolks to the wet mix and whisk together.

Whip the whites into soft peaks with the whisk.

Pour the wet mix into the dry mix.

Gently combine.

Fold the egg whites into the batter in thirds.

Grease and heat the waffle iron.

Pour 1 cup of batter onto the hot and ready iron.

Cook for 3 minutes on each side or until the waffle is golden brown and lightly charred.

Remove the waffle from the iron; immediately brush it with butter and dust it with the cinnamon sugar mix.

Eat hot.

## INGREDIENTS

### DRY

¼ cup pastry flour (low protein)

¾ cup einkorn flour

2 tablespoons sugar

¼ teaspoon salt

### WET

1 cup whole milk, room temperature

3 tablespoons vegetable oil

2 eggs, room temperature

Butter

Cinnamon sugar (2 tablespoons each fine sugar and cinnamon, combined)

## TOOLS YOU'LL NEED

Measuring cups and spoons

2 medium-size bowls

Whisk

2 small bowls

Large wooden spoon

Butter or grease for the waffle iron

Campfire waffle iron

# SPELT WAFFLES

Makes about 8 waffles

Aromatic and toothy like a bouquet of honey and flowers. Warming, fattening, and strengthening, a good start to the day. Dust with bee pollen.

Ready the coals (page 47).

In a medium bowl, sift together the flours, sugar, and salt. Set the bowl aside.

In a separate medium bowl, whisk together the milk and vegetable oil.

Separate the eggs into the small bowls.

Add the yolks to the wet mix and whisk together.

Whip the whites into soft peaks with the whisk.

Pour the wet mix into the dry mix.

Gently combine.

Fold the egg whites into the batter in thirds.

Grease and heat the waffle iron.

Pour 1 cup of batter onto the hot and ready iron.

Cook for 3 minutes on each side or until the waffle is golden brown and lightly charred.

Regrease the skillet as needed.

Eat hot, covered in butter and maple syrup, and dusted with bee pollen.

### INGREDIENTS

**DRY**

¼ cup pastry flour (low protein)

¾ cup spelt flour

2 tablespoons sugar

¼ teaspoon salt

**WET**

1 cup whole milk, room temperature

3 tablespoons vegetable oil

2 eggs, room temperature

Butter

Maple syrup

Bee pollen

### TOOLS YOU'LL NEED

Measuring cups and spoons

2 medium-size bowls

Whisk

2 small bowls

Large wooden spoon

Butter or grease for the waffle iron

Campfire waffle iron

# LUMBERJACK DELIGHT

Makes about 8 waffles

Gritty and sturdy, these waffles will get you through a few hours at the chopping block. Dust with bee pollen.

Ready the coals (page 47).

In a medium bowl, sift together the flours, sugar, and salt. Set aside.

In a separate medium bowl, whisk together the milk and vegetable oil.

Separate the eggs into the small bowls.

Add the yolks to the wet mix and whisk together.

Whip the whites into soft peaks with the whisk.

Pour the wet mix into the dry mix.

Gently combine.

Fold the egg whites into the batter in thirds.

Grease and heat the waffle iron.

Pour 1 cup of batter onto the hot and ready iron.

Cook for 3 minutes on each side or until the waffle is golden brown and lightly charred.

Regrease the skillet as needed.

Eat hot, covered in butter and maple syrup.

## INGREDIENTS

**DRY**

⅓ cup white wheat flour

⅓ cup rye flour

¼ cup buckwheat flour

2 tablespoons sugar

¼ teaspoon salt

**WET**

1 cup whole milk, room temperature

3 tablespoons vegetable oil

2 eggs, room temperature

Butter

Maple syrup

Bee pollen

## TOOLS YOU'LL NEED

Measuring cups and spoons

2 medium-size bowls

Whisk

2 small bowls

Large wooden spoon

Butter or grease for the waffle iron

Campfire waffle iron

MAY

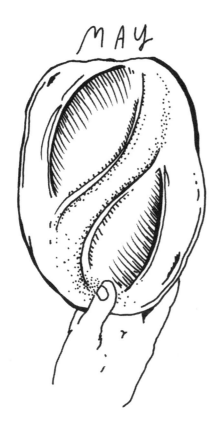

Good bread comes from the place where joy and sorrow meet.
—posted may 21

Pulled from the ether, the bakery lay kicking and screaming at my feet. Self-indulgent days of pity were numbered. Cultures fermenting. Wood stacked. Oven hot. Fresh rhythms of life established themselves along with weeds in the garden. The smell of bread was resurrected over the hillside to the sound of cattle giving birth. The early dawn hours found me sloshing in buckets of bread. Elbow deep in dough, I surrendered. The only machine in the bakery was an old food processor for pulsing herbs. Lining up giant tubs, I mixed by hand down the bench one dough at a time, reciting an ancient language.

We know how to make bread deep in our being. That is why it calls to us. The labor is the labor of coming home. The fragrance of flour passing between two stones and the suppleness of bubbling dough wake us to intuitive knowledge. It is important to relax the classifying mind while baking. Engage with the dough in front of you, not the idea of it. Work with a loving attitude. To love in baking is to remain present. Herein lies the health benefit: the practice of caring. The quality of care you can extend to the bread is related to the quality of care you provide yourself.

## HOW TO MAKE BREAD

Bread is a mix of flour and water, activated with leaven and controlled by salt, fermented and baked in a hot environment. Not much more than four ingredients are necessary to create a pleasing loaf. I mix one base dough, the Ploughman, adding in black pepper, herbs, olive oil, and seeds for variation when the salt is incorporated. Learning one simple dough well and practicing it repeatedly will lead to swift progress.

If you are new to bread, you will need to follow a time line until you develop your intuition. Once you grasp the overall process, it becomes apparent that at any juncture you could choose from several courses of action. As you gain experience, muscle memory will develop, and your senses will guide you. What this tells us is that bread making is flexible, not rigid. Bakers strive for correct textures, smells, and tastes regardless of what the formula says. Let's talk about the basics first, and then we'll explore the recipe itself. . . .

### Culture.
What I refer to as the culture is the base mixture of flour, water, wild yeast, and bacteria that is maintained and refreshed.

**Leaven.**

Leaven is a separate and/or larger mix of culture, flour, and water that goes directly into the bread. Creating a leaven allows for experimentation in flour types, hydration levels, and fermentation times without endangering the root mixture of yeast and bacteria.

A liquid leaven is equal parts flour and water. It ferments quickly, is comfortable to mix by hand, and dissolves easily in water. Liquid leavens encourage bacterial growth, imparting a milky, floral quality that balances the acidity that develops in long, overnight fermentations. When started with a healthy culture, a liquid leaven may be usable in as little as two hours. Lengthening the fermentation pulls out a pungent flavor. I use mine at the eight-hour mark. The leaven is ready when it has a bubbly surface and has doubled in volume. It should smell yogurt-like and fresh. Drop a thumbnail piece into water: if it floats, you're good to go.

**The flour, the water, and salt.**

The Ploughman is made here at the bakery using type 75 bread flour from Carolina Ground. The "75" refers to the sifted nature of the flour—25 percent of the overall bran was removed in the bolter. This flour is generally milled from a hard red winter wheat and I often blend it 50/50 with flour made from a soft red winter wheat, honoring the kind of grain the South is known for. The blending of the fours makes the bread structurally sound while lending a creamy texture to the crumb. You may order both flours online from www.carolinaground.com or use any reputable bread flour from your region.

Water that you would drink is fine for our purposes here, although steer away from chlorinated water. The amount of water, or hydration, in this recipe is 75 percent. The resulting dough will be wet enough to have a pleasing, custard-like crumb, but stiff enough that shaping isn't a nightmare for the beginner. As your comfort level improves, increase the hydration for a looser dough and more open crumb. I use pink sea salt in the bakery, but most salt will do. If the only salt accessible is large, coarse crystal, dissolve it in a little warm water first.

## Hand mixing.

This bread is intended to be mixed by hand. The goal is to bring together a dough with as little work as possible, meaning that each pinch, stroke, fold, or squeeze must be done with confidence and intentionality. Use firm, whole body motions. Your arms are your tools. The way you hold your body while making bread has very direct results in the overall volume, shape, and interior structure.

Keep a sense of mindfulness about yourself. Are your feet rooted on the floor? Are you breathing? Commit to the motion and follow through. Hesitating while handling dough causes inefficiencies; doubt sets in, and your hands linger, fusing to the bread. The difficulty of mixing or shaping, once flustered, only increases. Anticipate each step, and when you begin, sink into your body and let it do the work. The cleanliness of your hands is a representation of the focused nature of your mind and the relaxed quality of your body.

## Temperature.

Our goal is a dough with final temperature between 75 and 77 degrees Fahrenheit. This climate promotes the growth of strength and flavor in tandem. Too warm, and the bacterial benefits are hindered; too cold, and the yeast struggles to gain momentum. Imagine the bread as your body. What kind of bath would you like to get into? If it's cool, add warm water. If it's hot out, add cool water. Lukewarm water is suitable in most situations.

**A word about baskets.**

The forms and materials you use to proof your bread with can have noticeable effects on the final crumb and volume. I prefer using simple wicker baskets that can be purchased cheaply from restaurant supply companies. They typically come in sets of twelve and referred to as bread baskets, often used for rolls and butter in a table setting. I use cut-up flour sack towels to drape inside the baskets. You may use a variety of materials to line the baskets as long as they don't have an excess of lint. Over time, a crust will build up on the cloths. I prefer this, it's like seasoning on a cast-iron skillet. I only launder them once a year. Use your bench knife to scrape cloths clean after each use.

**When to start.**

Think backward from when you want your bread to be baked. Let's assume a bake on Saturday night (if you bake your loaves as soon as they're proofed) or Sunday morning (if you refrigerate them overnight before baking): remove your culture from refrigeration and refresh it on Friday morning and Friday afternoon (Remember: if it has been in the fridge for weeks, it might need more refreshments). Friday night, before bed, mix the leaven as described in the following section, then refresh the leftover culture and return it to the fridge after a few hours. (Details on how to refresh your culture are on page 24.)

# THE PLOUGHMAN

Makes 4 loaves of bread

I've been making this bread weekly for five years using various flours and adjusting the leaven and hydration to my mood and the weather. A country sour with a medium crumb and thick crust, it's perfect to take into the field for lunch or toast for breakfast in a frying pan with butter. Creating more than one loaf at a time is the best way to learn; share and stock up the freezer.

Bakers think of each ingredient in relation to the weight of the flour in a formula. Flour is always at 100 percent. So, for example, the flour in this formula is 1684 grams and the water is 1263 grams, so the water is said to be 75 percent of the weight of the flour. This makes bread formulas easy to adjust and scale with some simple math and a little practice.

*About 24 to 36 hours before baking (depending on whether you plan to rest the proofed loaves overnight)*, make the leaven. Pour 62 grams of your active culture into a medium bowl, along with the 250 grams each bread flour and lukewarm water. Cover. Let ferment overnight.

*The next day*, choose a place to mix where you can lean over your workspace with ease. Using a digital scale, weigh the flour into a large bowl with deep sides. Aerate it with your fingers by tossing it together for a moment. Set aside. Weigh the water into a separate large bowl. Add the leaven to the water and stir to combine. The leaven will first float on the surface, become stringy as you stir, and eventually fully dissolve. Pour the slurry into the flour. Keep your fingers together in a curved paddle shape and fold the dough over itself by working your hand directly under the dough, lifting and stretching it up, and then quickly turning your wrist to bring the elongated swath of dough over itself and connected to the opposite side. It's a

## INGREDIENTS

**FOR THE LEAVEN**

100% bread flour 187g

100% water 187g

25% culture 47g

*Total weight: 421g*

**FOR THE DOUGH**

100% bread flour 1684g

75% water 1263g

35% leaven 421g

2% salt 34g

*Total weight: 3402g*

## TOOLS YOU'LL NEED

Digital scale

Medium-size mixing bowl

2 large mixing bowls

Wooden spoon

Bench knife

Dusting flour

4 hand towels

Well-oiled 9-inch loaf pan

3 flour-dusted, cloth-lined baskets

swoop underneath, a quick pull up, and an ambitious flip of the wrist. Repeat this motion, rotating the bowl, until the dough has fully pulled away from the sides and formed into a loose ball. Use a bench knife to scrape down the sides of the bowl and underneath the dough. The dough will be shaggy and tacky at first, but with a short rest and the addition of salt, it will become smooth and malleable. Toss the salt evenly across the surface of the bread. Cover.

Allow the dough to rest for 30 minutes without working in the salt. Salt has a tightening effect on the gluten and also inhibits fermentation. During this grace time, known as an autolyse, the dough fully hydrates and the gluten gathers strength while enzymatic activity comes alive.

After the autolyse begin to pinch in the salt. Hold your hands like crab claws. Starting closest to your body, gather the dough between your "pinchers" and work away from you to the opposite side of the bowl, firmly squeezing and releasing the dough like a rope between your hands. The salt will dissolve, and you will immediately feel the bread take on a sense of tension. Once there is no trace of salt, cover and let it rest for another 30 minutes.

The bread is now entering bulk fermentation. This can last 4 to 5 hours, in which time the dough is given a series of folds. During bulk fermentation, the dough will rise in volume and begin to feel lofty, exhibiting bubbles here and there on the surface and loosening in structure.

A fold consists of lifting and stretching the dough up and across itself to the opposite side of the container, in a series for four turns, making a ball of dough in the middle of the vessel. Folding regulates temperature and builds strength. Use your whole hand, not just your fingertips, to lift, stretch, and flip the dough. This builds elasticity, providing volume in the final loaf. Fold 30 minutes after incorporating the salt and then every hour on the hour. You may divide your dough within 45 minutes of the final fold if it is relaxed enough. Test the strength of your dough by pulling a little away with the tip of your finger. Does it make a bubblegum-like window or shred apart? If the dough isn't coming together and remains loose, increase the number of folds. It is

**FOLDS WITH AN ACTIVE DOUGH DESIRED TO SHAPE IN 4 HOURS:**

- Dough mixed at 9 A.M.
- 30-minute autolyse
- Salt added at 9:30 A.M.
- First fold at 10 A.M.
- Second fold at 11 A.M.
- Third fold at noon
- Divide and preshape at 1 P.M.
- 10- to 30-minute bench rest
- Final shape at 1:30 P.M.

possible to fold the dough without building strength: this happens from a weak and unsure touch. Be forceful, deliberate, and use some elbow grease!

When it's time to divide the dough, turn it out onto a clean surface dusted lightly with flour. Using both hands, gently lift and stretch the right edge of the dough to the middle. Gently lift and stretch the left side toward the middle. Repeat the same motions from the top edge down toward the center and from the bottom edge up toward the center. The dough will go from a wiggly mass to a taut rectangle with a "skin" now stretched on the surface. Lightly dust with flour.

Eyeball the rectangle into four equal-sized portions. At this point, imagine the bench knife is fused into your dominant hand. Use the bench knife to cut, lift, and place your dough where it needs to be, keeping your free hand away as much as possible. Overhandling at this stage can degas the delicate dough. If your hands get stuck in the bread, stop. Wash them. Scrape and clean up your work area. Start again. Divide with a swift cutting and separating rather than a sawing motion. Use the scale to check each loaf at 30 ounces.

The goal of a preshape is to set up the dough structurally for its final form. Through a series of stretches, tucks, and rolls, the inside of the bread is defined under a gluten cloak. The dough should be able to move freely on the table. Take care to use the least amount of flour in your work area to achieve this. Gently pat a piece of dough into a rectangle. Lift the bottom edge up and press it into the loaf two-thirds of the way up. You will now be looking at a bulge of dough with a lip at the top. Take the sides, stretch them gently and bring them to cross over the center of the dough. The dough will now look like an open envelope. With gusto, take the bottom edge and flip it up to meet the top lip, sealing the dough into a cylinder. Repeat with the other three loaves. Let them rest, covered with cloth, for 10 to 30 minutes.

Using a bench knife, flip over a preform and gently pat it into a rectangle. Again take the bottom edge and fold it two-thirds of the way up the loaf. Gently stretch the sides and bring them to cross over the center of the dough. More overlap here will provide a nice core of tension so the bread maintains its shape during the final proof. Flip the bottom edge up to meet the top lip and tuck the dough into itself, beginning with a fair amount of tension and easing up as you finish. This last step is a micro movement with your wrists. Use caution and work quickly, never tearing the dough and keeping your fingers on the outside of the loaf.

You will now have a taut cylinder with a long seam running underneath and a smooth top. Pinch the ends. Lift the loaf with your bench knife and place it seam-side down into an oiled pan. Repeat the same shaping for the remaining three loaves, but transfer them seam-side up into flour dusted, cloth-lined baskets.

Proofing is the final stage of fermentation. The dough will rise and relax from the tension introduced while shaping. Initial proofing can last anywhere from 2 to 4 hours, depending on how fast the dough was moving in bulk fermentation and the ambient temperatures of the room. To test if the bread is fully proofed, poke the center of the loaf. If it springs back immediately, give it more time. If it holds the imprint of your finger with just a little spring, it's ready. Once proofed, you may either place your loaves, covered, in the fridge overnight or prepare your oven for baking (see Baking Loaves from a Basket, page 67, or Stenciled Loaves in a Pan, page 71).

Retarding your bread in refrigeration will slow down fermentation, adding complexity to the flavor profile. I do not go past 19 hours in cold storage, with room-temperature proofing between 1 and 3 hours. Even if you do not plan on retarding overnight, at least 20 minutes in refrigeration encourages the loaf to contract, making handling and scoring easier.

# BREADFARM SPRING 07

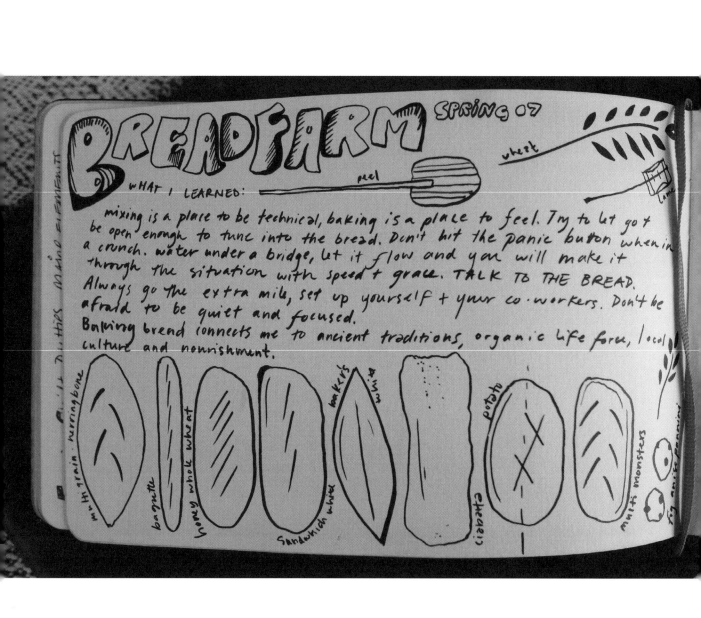

peel

wheat

lame

**WHAT I LEARNED:**

mixing is a place to be technical, baking is a place to feel. Try to let go + be open enough to tune into the bread. Don't hit the panic button when in a crunch. water under a bridge, let it flow and you will make it through the situation with speed + grace. TALK TO THE BREAD. Always go the extra mile, set up yourself + your co-workers. Don't be afraid to be quiet and focused. Baking bread connects me to ancient traditions, organic life force, local culture and nourishment.

multi grain · herringbone

baguette

honey whole wheat

sandwich whirl

baker's mild

ciabatta

potato

multi monsters

fig anise fennini

# BAKING LOAVES FROM A BASKET

Let go of appearances. Be concerned with more than just looks to achieve a bread that doesn't leave the heart bitter and the stomach empty. A respectable loaf of bread is not necessarily visually perfect. Bread should look, first and foremost, like it came from somewhere. The grain from a particular farm, the water from a certain well. Be proud of your work and understand that bread is as much a practice as it is a noun.

**TOOLS YOU'LL NEED**

5-quart Dutch oven

Double-sided razor and a wooden coffee stirer

Parchment (not waxed)

Potholders

Timer

Wire rack

Remove the racks in your oven so that you have a single rack in the middle. On this rack place your covered Dutch oven. Turn the oven on to 500 degrees. Preheating the Dutch oven mimics the hot masonry found in a wood-fired oven, ensuring a nice oven spring.

When the oven has fully heated, remove one of the loaves from refrigeration to bake. The others can remain chilled until it's their turn. Next you will turn out the loaves and score, or slash, them using a tool called a lame (pronounced LAHM)—French for "blade"—which is a long stick that holds a sharp razor. Make your own by sliding the double-sided razor onto the end of the coffee stirrer.

Before you proceed, consider the angle, depth, and pattern of your score. This will influence the final appearance and taste of your bread. As the flap of dough created by your slash pulls back and away from the bread in the heat of the oven, it begins to bake prior to the rest of the loaf. This creates a range of color, which translates to a range of flavor. The direction of your score will have an effect on how it opens. One long slash down the middle encourages the loaf to spread, while several short cuts will help maintain the original form.

You may wish to adjust the depth of your score based on the proofing. If underproofed, score heavy. If overproofed, score lightly. On a perfectly proofed loaf of bread, the score should stay within the "skin" of the loaf, going less than ½ inch into the body of the bread. Imagine a center line running down the middle of the loaf. Orient all slashes toward this line, going for long sweeping strokes with even depth. Hold your blade at a 45-degree angle, never straight up and down.

Flip the bread out onto a piece of parchment paper, aiming for the middle. Quickly pull away the cloth and basket, and set them aside. Score the loaf.

Carefully remove the Dutch oven. It will be heavy and hot, so use caution. Remove the lid.

Pick up the parchment holding the bread and lower it into the waiting pot. Push the parchment away from the loaf, toward the walls of the pot. Place the lid securely back on and return the pot to the oven for 20 minutes. Leaving the lid on for the first 20 minutes of baking traps the moisture released from the bread against itself, promoting a graceful unfolding of scores.

Twenty minutes into baking, reduce the oven temperature to 450 degrees and remove the lid from the Dutch oven. Hot steam will pour out, so exercise caution. Finish baking for another 15 to 20 minutes.

When done, your loaf will have a glossy, mahogany hue and, if tapped on the bottom, will sound hollow. Rest it on a wire rack, allowing air to circulate around the entire crust. Cool it for 2 to 3 hours before slicing if you wish to taste the true flavor. Listen for the sounds of cracking: the cooling interior pulls against the crust, making hairline fractures into a chorus.

To properly store a loaf, place the cut side down on your cutting board or keep it wrapped in a cloth like linen or heavy canvas inside a paper bag. Your bread will keep 4 to 5 days. To freeze it, slice the entire loaf once it's cool, seal it inside a gallon freezer bag, and take it out one slice at a time, toasting to refresh.

# STENCILED LOAVES IN A PAN

In a time when individual homes lacked kitchens, bread was baked in communal ovens. It was necessary then to have a stencil or signature to your bread to distinguish whose was whose when loaves were pulled from the hearth. Nature, family crests, personal hobbies, and moon cycles are just a few places to draw inspiration from when creating your own stencil. I like to take a walk by the river before I start.

**TOOLS YOU'LL NEED**

Firm piece of paper such as a file folder or Bristol board

Pen or pencil

X-Acto knife with a fresh blade

Self-healing cutting mat

Flour sifter

1 cup flour

Kitchen towel

Sheet pan with raised sides

Preheat the oven to 475 degrees and arrange the racks so that one is in the center of the oven and another is just below it.

Cut a rectangle of firm paper to match the surface area of the 9-inch loaf pan. Using a pen or pencil, mark a ½-inch border around the outside of the paper. Draw your chosen design, focusing on the center strip of the stencil. Once the loaf has risen, your design will be more detailed in the center and diffuse on the outer edges, so keep this in mind. Using the X-Acto knife and self-healing mat, cut the design out.

Place the stencil on top of the loaf. Fill the sifter with flour and evenly sift back and forth over the paper. You only need a light dusting to make your image appear. Too much flour will burn and create a dry mouthful. Set aside the sifter and remove the stencil, lifting directly up so as to not spill the flour.

When baking with a Dutch oven, the moisture released from the bread is held close to the skin, providing ample steam, yet here you must provide the steam separately. Steam softens the skin of the bread and reduces tears and blowouts. To steam: soak the kitchen towel in water, place it in the sheet pan, and position it on the bottom rack underneath the bread when you put the loaf in to bake. Remove the pan with the towel 15 minutes into the bake. Bake for a total of 25 to 30 minutes, or until it is ruby red and done. Remove the bread from the pan as soon as it comes out of the oven, and cool it on a wire rack for between 1 and 2 hours to taste the full flavor.

*We are a movement. We are a motion. We are unfurling before you.*
*— posted June 14*

We often don't ask for help until our hands are tied behind our back. If making bread is a solitary, mindful self-expression, then pizza is a noisy journey into community and the mess of human relationships. Pizza nights at the bakery started innocently enough. And they began like this: Light fire at 6:00 A.M. Mix dough. Prep vegetables. Fold dough. Make Yard Sauce. Shape dough. Let rest. Do dishes. Slice cheese. Dough goes to the cooler. Feed oven wood. Bring out folding table and tablecloths. String bungee cords.

Dot with clothespins. Chalkboard. Chalk. Write. Cut pie boxes for tickets. Get pens. Get cash box. Find spare change. Throw quilts around the yard. Set up campfire. Put out trash cans and recycling. Fold 60 pizza boxes. Stamp each box. Cutting boards and pizza cutter in place. Light candles. Toppings and dough into place. Cue music. Pour stiff drink. Drink. Take picture. Post to Instagram. Light campfire. 6:00 P.M. Wait.

The time between posting an image of the raging fire to the all-seeing, all-knowing Internet and the arrival of the first actual person was torture. I went through every phase of second-guessing. Staring at the homespun ticket line littered with clothespins, I calmed myself by repeating: "I'm just playing." I hadn't felt like this since I was twelve, on my bike, pedaling far from home.

A core group of friends arose to help when pizza night got too big for my own two hands. I found a deep joy in sharing my rituals. What had saved me was the idea that I could do anything alone. What was going to propel life into something meaningful was sharing the burden. Taking orders, making change, and working the oven were delegated according to comfort levels and expertise. My task was to top the pizzas and pass them off into the flames.

The magic of pizza is watching it cook right in front of you. A 715-degree fire animates the chamber while the pizza bakes two feet in front of the fire, jerking and heaving like it's rising from the dead. The dough bubbles, turning into a ruby crust with tiny blisters, a little charred. The cheese perfectly melts and browns. Seared toppings. Hot. Crispy. Chewy. Salty. Nutty. Sour. Tossed onto a wooden cutting board. Eaten within minutes.

The power of staying with something is the potential of recognition. The bakery received press that exposed us to the eye of those whose job it was to regulate and oversee matters of culinary safety. The mailman flagged me down on a hot afternoon with a green envelope in his hand. He looked at me and apologized.

I looked down at an official letter from the health department stating that my business was in danger. I called the number, and a kind woman told me I should stick with my apple pies. Campfires, knives, and illegal drinking rubbed them the wrong way. Now you can carry on pizza night. Make the dough. Prep the toppings. Heat the oven. Call your friends. Pour a drink. Take a moment to wait. And then, of course, turn up the music and boogie.

# SUNDAY-NIGHT PIZZA PARTY

Makes 4 10-inch pizzas

This process assumes a Sunday night gathering—simply adjust as needed for any other day. Remove your culture from refrigeration. Refresh on Friday morning and Friday afternoon. Mix the active culture into the leaven prior to turning in. Cover and let ferment. I use a 50/50 blend of Carolina Ground type 75 bread and pastry flour to create an all-purpose flour. Tender, extensible, and chewy are the qualities I go for in a crust. If you're feeling adventuresome, fresh spelt flour makes an incredible crust!

Good pizza dough can be made with good bread dough. Follow the process for bread making on pages 61 to 63, all the way through dividing, with one variation: add the glugs of olive oil when you add the slurry of water and leaven.

*The day before baking.* Scale the dough into four portions around 255 grams each on a lightly floured surface. To make a round, cup your hand in a "C" shape and roll the dough against the table in a clockwise motion, allowing a little of the dough to stick to the table while the rest tightens. When done, the skin of the dough should be continuous and taut, with the body of the dough slightly lifted away from the table. Dust the bottom of an airtight container (large enough for your rounds) with a little flour. Stagger doughs an inch apart. They will relax over time, spreading somewhat. Cover. Let the dough rise at room temp for 1 hour. (Longer in cool weather, shorter in warm weather.) Transfer it to refrigeration. Flavor will develop substantially in refrigeration, yet at some point the dough will break down structurally. This happens at around 72 hours, depending on the storage temperature. I hold my dough at 48 degrees for 24 hours.

## INGREDIENTS

**FOR THE LEAVEN**

100% bread flour 65g

100% water 65g

25% starter 16g

*Total weight: 147g*

**FOR THE DOUGH**

100% bread flour 595g

65% water 383g

25% leaven 147g

2% salt 12g

A few glugs of olive oil

*Total weight: 1137g*

**FOR THE PIZZA**

Yard Sauce (recipe on page 81)

8 ounces mozzarella (227 grams)

Toppings of your choice (see sidebar on page 82 for some of my favorite combinations)

## TOOLS YOU'LL NEED

Digital scale

Medium-size mixing bowl

2 large mixing bowls

Dusting flour for shaping

Bench knife

Large airtight container

Pizza stone

50/50 blend of cornmeal and all-purpose flour (½ cup each)

Peel or parchment paper

Large spoon

Wire rack

Pizza cutter

*One hour prior to baking.* Remove the dough from the refrigerator and let it warm to room temperature.

*To bake the pizzas.* Remove extra oven racks, positioning just one in the middle of the oven chamber. Set in the baking stone. Preheat to 500 degrees, or as hot as your oven will go. Allow the stone to thoroughly heat; this will give your pizza a nice lift. To test the temperature, toss a pinch of the cornmeal/flour blend onto the surface. If the stone is ready, it should brown within 15 seconds.

Dust the peel with the blend of cornmeal and flour. Wooden peels stay cooler longer and are great for preparing pizzas during a party, yet the thin edge on metal peels makes removal from the oven a breeze. I use whatever is on hand. Parchment paper is suitable for this activity. It is more about understanding the dynamics and the desired effect than it is about having the nicest tools.

Scoop the dough up with the bench knife. Flip it onto the floured peel so that the top is now the bottom. Gently indent a ring ¼ inch from the edge. Making two fists, go under the dough so it's now resting on top of your knuckles. Use the backs of your hands to stretch the dough in opposite directions, working toward the rim. Now work the outer edges, letting the dough hang while you roll it over the backs of your hands. Gravity will do much of the work.

Return the dough round to the peel. If you have any small holes, pinch them together and carry on. Work quickly and with a delicate touch.

Drizzle a large spoonful of Yard Sauce over the doughy circle. Smear it toward the edges with the backside of the spoon. Top with 2 ounces (57g) fresh mozzarella. Add the toppings of your choice.

Give the peel a shimmy shake to make sure the pizza can slide off. If it's stuck, lift it with the bench knife and toss more cornmeal/flour underneath. Open the oven and slide the pizza onto the stone.

Bake the pizza for 10 to 12 minutes, depending on how strong the heat in your oven is. Broil for the last minute to get a blistery, caramelized crust. Use the peel to transfer the pizza from the oven to a wire rack. Let it cool for few minutes before moving it to a cutting board. Slice and share.

# YARD SAUCE

Yard Sauce is what I affectionately named the only dressing I use on pizza. I make it from olive oil, herbs, and wild edibles found around the bakery—rosemary, parsley, nettles, thyme, sage, oregano, lemon balm, dill, chickweed, cilantro, and wild onions have all made cameos. Tailor it to your taste. Plant an herb garden just for it!

You'll need a food processor for this recipe. Make it the day of the party.

Pick/gather the herbs.

Remove any stems or debris.

Rinse and let dry.

Peel the entire head of garlic and roughly chop it.

In the food processor, blend the olive oil, garlic, lemon juice, lemon zest, salt, and pepper.

Add the herbs.

Pulse for 2 to 3 minutes.

Add more oil to thin, if necessary. (It should be spreadable with a spoon.)

Pour the sauce into the waiting jar and cover.

It will naturally separate. Shake it with the lid on to reincorporate.

Dress the pizza by the spoonful.

**INGREDIENTS**

2 large handfuls fresh herbs

1 head of garlic

About 3 cups olive oil

Juice and zest of 1 lemon

1 teaspoon salt

1 teaspoon black pepper

**TOOLS YOU'LL NEED**

Small sieve or lemon juicer

Microplane grater

Chopping knife

Cutting board

Food processor

16-ounce glass jar

## FLOWERS

I learned to appreciate edible flowers through Evan Chender, the Culinary Gardener. Once a chef himself, Evan tends an eight-thousand-square-foot intensively grown garden that is nothing short of paradise. He is also gracious, taking orders and requests well after preferred harvesting deadlines. His offerings are unique: leaves and roots and shoots not typically grown on larger farms. I'd pop a succulent, jewel-toned leaf no bigger than my thumb into my mouth and taste cucumber, lime, and pepper. A cascade through the nose first, over the tongue, and then in the chest. Scatter flowers and delicate greens on a pizza after baking.

### TIPS

- Identify the flower.
- Make sure it's not poisonous.
- Do not consume flowers that have been sprayed by pesticides.
- Avoid roadside flowers and flowers from a commercial florist, garden, or nursery.
- Harvest and use flowers at peak bloom.
- Eat in moderation.
- Make your own floral confetti out of some of these blossoms: dandelion, fennel, dill, elderberry, honeysuckle, nasturtium, purslane, red clover, pansy, violet, geranium, snapdragon, and marigold.

### TOPPINGS

Think outside the box when it comes to choosing toppings. When pizza night began, we used whatever damaged or misshapen vegetables came out of the field. Now I go the farmers' market and fill up my grocery sack with whatever is new. Working with something like a potato or turnips, toss them in a few tablespoons of the Yard Sauce, and roast them on a sheet pan prior to using. Light and fresh greens are always added post-bake.

- Spinach, roasted turnips, and garlic scapes
- Roasted radishes, fresh herbs, and pea shoots
- Split romaine, anchovies, and lemon zest
- Tomatoes, basil, and sweet corn
- Roasted okra, Jimmy Nardello peppers, and prosciutto
- Peaches, red onion, capers, and chili flakes
- Figs, shallots, and Gruyère
- Thinly sliced roasted potatoes and sautéed fennel
- Cauliflower, leeks, and roasted garlic
- Thinly sliced roasted sweet potato and caramelized onions

JULY

I waited forever for you to show up. Now I'll wait forever for you to come back.
— posted July 7

*Friday, July 1, 4 A.M. Bake pies for Laura and Jason's wedding. Load oven with wood and kindling. Light. Measure dry ingredients. Cube cold butter. Hand mix pie dough. Cover and chill. Chop peaches. Toss blueberries. Zest twenty lemons. Whisk heavy cream and egg yolks. Bring out dough. Roll. Cut. Transfer into tins. Press and trim. Fill. Top. Brush with egg wash. Roll out scrap dough. Design and score shapes. Embellish pies. Egg wash again. Dust with coarse sugar. Vent. Chill. Rake coals from oven chamber. Mop out oven. Close oven door. Do dishes. Clean sinks. Dust. Sweep. Mop. Line sheet pans with parchment. Open oven. Transfer pies to sheet pans. Carry outside. Load. Close. Fold boxes. Stamp. Line with parchment. Take out pies. Cool. Box. Close. Tie with string.*

I was alone through every season by the time Jason and Laura's wedding rolled around, and I noticed how particular I was becoming. My whole world arranged in just the right order. Never a stray water glass. Never a shoe out of line. Never a hair on the sink. Never a shirt on the floor. Everything was immaculate. Everything was frozen. I had control of my life, but I was also suffocating it. So when I saw his shoes tossed by the woodstove and his beer sweating water on the windowsill I got nervous.

We'd met the month before, when his truck broke down in my driveway. A stray member of Jason's bachelor party, he was trying to leave the neighborhood after a weekend on the river. Seems fate had other plans. Standing in the house, I saw him milling around the mailbox, and I stepped out on the porch to see what the issue was. He was silhouetted in the afternoon sun; I sized him up according to the outline of his body.

It would take a week to repair the engine, so Laura and Jason temporarily got a roommate, and I was ousted from my formal role as a third wheel. I immediately assessed that we were from different worlds, that I didn't enjoy his taste in music—and when he said he didn't like cake, any possible interest I had evaporated like water on hot pavement. Until the last night of his detour. We had a popcorn-and-movie night at my house, and I picked out my favorite film concerning witches, prideful conceit, and exile. Jason and Laura trailed off, but the film held his interest, and when he opened his mouth and started talking about the symbolism of the chalice and the goat, my neck broke turning to look at him. He was bathed in a flickering blue glow and I thought, *I've been waiting my whole life to talk to this man.* And then, as the credits rolled, I kicked him out and locked the door.

Two weeks later, I told Laura he could stay at my house during the wedding, and at 1 A.M. on the first of July, he let himself in and disappeared, along with his dog, into the guest room. Lunch came and went, and I still had twelve chess pies left to bake. The wood-fired oven would have scorched them, so I cranked on the kitchen stove. I showered. Slipped on my favorite dress. Laced up an apron. Put on Billie Holiday and set to work. Melted the butter. Let it cool. Measured the flour, sugar, and cornmeal. Whisked the buttermilk, eggs, and vanilla. Folded the wet into the dry in three parts. Got out the beans. Cut parchment circles. Blind-baked the bottom shells and lined them with fresh fruit.

I didn't notice him at first, leaning in the doorway. Without his shirt on. I hadn't had a feeling from the waist down in years, and I couldn't tell if I was experiencing attraction or food poisoning. I had wanted to be a nun ever since I was girl, and my current celibate streak was a source of pride. I thought, *This is temptation. Resist.* What would help? A rule. A rule would help. Raising a dripping whisk, I announced that visitors were required to wear shirts at all times. He didn't budge. Instead he suggested that he was actually going to take off all his clothes and get in the shower. Pouring the custard into the pie shells, my hands were shaking. *We have other rules here, too,* I said, *like you can't watch me do this.*

The pies found their way into the oven, and he managed to locate the shower. I went outside to fumble under the potting table for a pack of cigarettes I kept for emergencies. Pacing back and forth, I had one. And then another. He emerged fresh onto the patio with a furrowed brow. It appeared he didn't have a date to the rehearsal dinner. My phone rang. Laura said there was a cancelation and suddenly extra room at the table. I told her I'd just put her very important pies in the oven. *Just get here when you can,* she said, and hung up. *Looks like you need a ride to dinner and I need a date,* he said. I looked up to meet his gaze: *How do you feel about being late?*

We sat in front of the oven watching the pies bake and played twenty-one questions. It was the longest hour of my life. The timer popped, and I scrambled to my feet, opening the oven door. A wave of warm milk and raspberry flooded the kitchen. We boxed jiggly pies, not waiting for them to cool, and ran out the door. Pulling bobby pins out of my hair, I tossed my apron on the woodpile and climbed into his truck. We rolled down the windows and turned up the Beach Boys. Speeding toward the lights of town, my arm out the window, a trail of dust clouding the taillights: for once, I'd left the kitchen without sweeping.

## HOW TO MAKE A PIE THE BEST WAY

Everyone wants to know how to make the flakiest pie crust, but the reality is that there are many different ways a light dough can be achieved and experienced. The texture of pie dough can range from mealy to flaky. Mealy dough has a lower percentage of liquid, holding up well against filling with substantial juices or eggs. Flaky dough puffs considerably and shatters when bitten. In the middle is a sandy-textured, crumbly crust. Each kind of dough has its place depending on the filling and amount of detail you wish to impart in any design work. Firm doughs support decorative aspects, holding shapes and clean lines. Flaky doughs make excellent free-form galettes and open-faced tarts. Regardless, when baked, a good crust should be golden, shiny, and deeply browned.

### Flour.
Source flour with a protein content of 10 percent or lower. I choose the Carolina Ground type 75 pastry flour for a provincial taste or the Crema pastry flour, also from Carolina Ground, for a crisp texture. Both are made from a soft, red winter wheat. Start with cold flour. I store mine in the freezer.

## Fat.

Every fat has a different melting point. Shortening is a favorite amongst pie bakers because it has a very high melting point. However, shortening and/or lard can leave off-putting flavors for sweet pies and a filmy feel in the mouth. Butter has a lower melting point, yet a pleasant, milky, grassy character. I use an all-butter recipe that has an 82 percent butterfat content. I like to order in bulk from the local co-op. If you feel adventurous, try 80 percent butter to 20 percent lard.

European-style butters have a higher percentage of butterfat and are considered cultured butters, which means that the cream is somewhat fermented. This imparts a distinctly "buttery" taste. In today's butter, bacteria (Lactococcus and Leuconostoc) are introduced after the pasteurization process. The water in butter is released as steam while baking, giving pie dough a lift similar to puff pastry. Whatever butter you choose, be sure to keep it cold throughout the process so the water doesn't leach out. I cube my butter beforehand and freeze it, starting the process with frozen butter. Since salt is added in with the dry ingredients, be sure to use unsalted butter in your crust. Salted butter can be overpowering in a dough, but if it's all you have, go forward and simply omit the salt in the dry mix.

## Water.

Water is both inside the butter and poured directly into the dough. If the butter is worked into the dry ingredients too much, water will separate out, soaking the flour, and a dough will form without the required amount of liquid. This results in a brittle dough due to lack of gluten development. If the butter is barely worked in when water is added, the dough will form too much gluten, making a tough and elastic crust that will shrink and snap. In general, use as little water as possible to bring the dough into a workable consistency. Always use ice-cold water and make adjustments a tablespoon at a time. Any water that you would drink is fine to make a pie crust with, although stay clear of chlorinated water, if possible.

### Sugar.

A few tablespoons of unrefined sugar in the crust tenderizes the dough and promotes browning.

### Salt.

Salt preserves the crust and enhances flavors. I use sea salt from the co-op.

# SMOKE SIGNALS CRUSTS

I use various sifted, low-protein pastry flour from Carolina Ground for a light, crispy, and slightly sweet crust. All-purpose flour is fine to use as well. Omit the sugar for a basic and versatile tart dough good for savory affairs.

I fresh mill Bloody Butcher corn for my cornmeal crust. Try different colors and flavors of corn for a colorfully freckled crust. The cornmeal crust has a sturdy and sandy flake, perfect for chess pies.

*Day before:* Blend the flour (and cornmeal, if using), sugar, and salt by hand in an airtight container and freeze. Cube the butter into lima-bean-sized pieces and freeze, also in an airtight container.

*Morning of:* Fill a pitcher with water and ice. When hydrating the dough, use water from this pitcher.

*To begin:* Bring out all the ingredients. Measure the butter into the flour mixture in a medium bowl. Toss, coating the butter in flour. Pinch half of the butter cubes between your thumb and index finger, flattening them out, leaving the rest as is. Your goal is to streak portions of butter through the dough so you will still need some untouched, large bits for this rough lamination. Toss the butter repeatedly in the flour while working. It will be difficult at first, but soon the frozen butter will turn into a waxy, pliable substance. This is the perfect state of butter for a pie crust. Make sure the butter stays in this zone and does not turn greasy or wet. Do not overwork the butter. If it warms up at any point chill the dough till the butter is firm once again. This process should only take about five minutes.

Make a well in the middle of the flour and butter. Pour in the water. Toss the mix from the sides over the water and start to knead it together. Although an overworked pie dough may cause a tough texture, this is not likely to happen working by hand. In fact, the opposite is often true. Put some elbow grease into it. If you feel

## INGREDIENTS

### DOUBLE-CRUST PIE

2½ cups pastry flour (low protein)

2 tablespoons unrefined sugar

1 teaspoon salt

1 cup (2 sticks) cold unsalted butter

½ cup ice-cold water + more if needed

### SINGLE-CRUST PIE

1½ cups pastry flour (low protein)

1 tablespoon unrefined sugar

½ teaspoon salt

½ cup (1 stick) cold unsalted butter

¼ cup ice-cold water + more, if needed

### CORNMEAL CRUST PIE

1¼ cups pastry flour (low protein)

¼ cup cornmeal

1 tablespoon unrefined sugar

½ teaspoon salt

½ cup (1 stick) cold unsalted butter

¼ cup ice-cold water, plus more if needed

### FOR THE FINISH

1 egg yolk

1 tablespoon heavy cream

Coarse sugar for dusting

that your crust needs more water, add only 1 tablespoon at a time. Dip your fingers in the water to smooth out dry or cracked spots. When it's done, there will be no dry flour and the dough should still have visible large chunks of butter.

If you're making a single flaky pastry or cornmeal crust, press the dough into a disk. If you're making a double crust, divide and press it into two evenly portioned disks. Refrigerate the dough in plastic wrap for at least 30 minutes.

Lightly dust your work surface with flour. Remove one disk of dough from refrigeration and let it warm for a moment. Unlike other pie-crust directions, we are not concerned with rolling out a circle of dough. Gently use your hands to form the disk into a bit of a rectangle rather than a circle and imagine a line running horizontally through the center. Roll the dough outward from this equator in both directions: away from your body toward the top of your work surface and from the middle toward yourself. Be sure to roll all the way off the edge. Roll the dough as long as you can, then fold it in half and in half again. Rotate 90 degrees. Now roll on the diagonal, down the center and along the edges, to create a sheet of dough. Frequently use the pie tin to check your measurement. You need the sheet of dough to be just large enough to trace the pie tin on. Roll to a thickness of ⅛ inch.

Lay the pie tin down on the sheet of dough. Using the edge as a guide, trim the dough with a pastry wheel ½ inch around. Set aside the scrap dough. Make sure the circle is free from the table by gently scraping underneath it with a bench knife. Place your forearm down the center. Fold one side over your arm. Lift. Catch the hanging dough in your free hand. Lift the dough with your arm and center it over the pie tin. Lay it down. Press it into the bottom and sides of the tin, eliminating any air.

*For a single-crust pie*, tuck any excess dough under itself so it's flush with the rim and flute or fork to decorate. Using the tines of a fork, poke the bottom five or six times. Whisk the egg yolk and heavy cream, then brush the rim with egg wash and dust with coarse sugar. Freeze for 10 minutes. Proceed to blind-baking (detailed on page 97).

### TOOLS YOU'LL NEED

Measuring cups and spoons

2 medium-size airtight containers

Small water pitcher

Medium-size mixing bowl with deep sides

Bench knife

Flour for dusting

French rolling pin

9-inch pie tin

Pastry wheel

Fork

Small bowl

Whisk

Pastry brush

Knife

Sheet pan

Parchment paper

Plastic wrap

*For a double-crust pie,* trim the excess around the rim. Ball the scraps together with the previous leftover dough. Set it aside. If the kitchen is warm, refrigerate the extra dough.

If making a double crust pie, remove the second disk from refrigeration. Let it warm for a moment. Roll it out, repeating all the steps you used for the first round. Once you've got your filling in the bottom pie shell, lay the top crust squarely over the center. Going around the outside edge, tuck the crust underneath itself, flush with edge of the tin. Flute it with your fingers or crimp with a fork.

In a small bowl, whisk together the egg yolk and cream. Brush the mixture over the pie. Roll out any scraps and cut shapes like leaves or feathers using a pastry wheel. Position them on the crust. Brush them with the egg wash. Vent the pie with a knife or fork a few times. Dust it with coarse sugar. Freeze it for 20 minutes. Proceed to double-crust baking (see page 98), or bake as recipe directs.

## TIPS

There should be only enough flour in the work area so that the crust can glide. Keep your dough moving on the table constantly, flipping it to work one side after you've rolled for a minute on the other. Make sure the dough doesn't fuse with the work surface, causing the butter to tear through the rough layers you're creating. Apply even pressure with your rolling pin, going over the dough firmly, but gently. Rather than driving with huge force and plowing it into the table, roll over the crust with long, sweeping strokes, extending all the way from your hips. Roll from up your legs, through the shoulders and arms, and out the tips of your fingers.

If the dough is not lengthening, the butter has broken through underneath and it is stuck to the table. Gently pick it up, scrape the work surface clean, lightly dust it with flour, and flip the dough over. If the dough warms up at any point, refrigerate it on a parchment-lined sheet pan until it chills.

# BLIND BAKING

Any pie involving a custard, a particularly juicy fruit, or an unbaked filling will require a par-baked, or blind-baked crust.

INGREDIENTS

Single pastry or cornmeal pie crust, prepared as described on pages 94–95

TOOLS YOU'LL NEED

Parchment paper

3 cups dried beans

Heat-safe container

Preheat the oven to 375 degrees.

Remove the crust from the freezer and line it with parchment paper. (I cut my parchment paper into rounds and keep a stack in the pantry.) Fill it with the dried beans, pushing the beans up the sides and leaving the center shallow.

Bake the crust for 15 minutes. Remove it from the oven. Carefully lift out the parchment and beans. Pour the beans into the heat-safe container to cool. Toss or keep the parchment for future use.

Return the crust to the oven. Bake it 10 minutes longer if you need a lighter crust that will require further baking once the filling is added. Bake it for another 25 minutes (or till it's golden brown) for a completely baked shell. If you have issues with your crust shrinking while blind baking, be sure to let the dough rest prior to cutting it, and take care to use a pastry flour: even all-purpose flours can have too much elasticity.

# DOUBLE-CRUST BAKING

Position a rack in the center of the oven and preheat it to 425 degrees.

Line the sheet tray with parchment and position the pie on it. Transfer it to the hot oven, placing it on the center rack, in the middle. Bake it for 15 minutes. Reduce the heat to 375 degrees and continue baking for 30 to 40 minutes. If the crust begins to darken too much, cover it with tinfoil, but do remember that color equals flavor and let that baby brown! When baking in a regular home oven, I use the broiler on high for the final 3 minutes to give a slight char that is such a signature of the wood-fired look and taste. Monitor your oven and adjust baking times according to hot spots.

Cool the pie at room temperature for at least 2 hours. Follow specific serving instructions. I find pie tastes best the second day!

## INGREDIENTS

Double-crust pie, filled as desired, covered with the top crust, finished, and chilled as described on page 94

## TOOLS YOU'LL NEED

Sheet tray with rimmed sides

Parchment paper

Tinfoil

# BROKEN-DOWN BERRY PIE

Makes one 9-inch pie

They say you've got to break down before you break through, and sometimes the worst situations turn out to be the best. Bold, blue, and jammy, with a bite of tart apple. Serve chilled.

You will need: 1 single 9-inch pie crust, blind-baked (page 95).

Preheat the oven to 425 degrees.

Rinse and dry the fresh berries.

Peel and chop the apple in small chunks.

Combine all the filling ingredients in the saucepan.

Bring the mixture to a light boil.

If the filling is burning and searing, add slightly more water.

Turn down the heat and simmer, stirring frequently, until the filling is thick.

Let it cool.

Transfer the filling into the prepared pie shell.

Bake for 35 minutes.

Let the pie cool for 2 hours.

Refrigerate.

## INGREDIENTS

**FILLING**

8 ounces fresh blackberries

8 ounces fresh raspberries

8 ounces fresh blueberries

1 Granny Smith apple

1 cup unrefined sugar

¼ cup cornstarch

1 teaspoon vanilla

¼ teaspoon nutmeg

¾ teaspoon salt

Juice of 1 lemon

Zest of 1 lemon

5 tablespoons water + more to adjust

## TOOLS YOU'LL NEED

Digital scale

Measuring cups and spoons

Colander

Peeler

Cutting board

Knife

Microplane grater

Saucepan

Large wooden spoon

# CRUMBLE TOP

Makes enough to top one 9-inch pie

A classic choice if you're forgoing a top crust.

Cube the butter into lima bean-size chunks.

Mix the dry ingredients together in the medium-size bowl.

Cut in the butter with a fork or pastry blender till it comes together and crumbles.

Chill the mixture for at least 20 minutes in an airtight storage container prior to using.

**INGREDIENTS**

½ cup (1 stick) butter

1½ cups pastry flour (low protein)

¼ cup unrefined sugar

¼ cup brown sugar

¼ cup rolled oats

¼ teaspoon cinnamon

¼ teaspoon salt

**TOOLS YOU'LL NEED**

Measuring cups and spoons

Cutting board

Knife

Medium-size bowl

Fork or pastry blender

Airtight storage container

# PEACHES AND RHUBARB PIE

Makes one 9-inch pie

Sweet and tangy and a little out of the box. Just like my new crush.

You will need: 1 single 9-inch pie crust, blind-baked (page 97), and Crumble Top (page 101).

Preheat the oven to 425 degrees.

Rinse the peaches and rhubarb.

Pit and slice the peaches, leaving the skins on.

Cut the ends off the rhubarb and chop the stalks into thick slices.

Combine all the filling ingredients in the saucepan.

Bring the mixture to a boil, stirring frequently with the wooden spoon.

If the filling is burning and searing, add slightly more water.

Turn down the heat to low.

Keep cooking and stirring until the mixture is thick.

Let it cool.

Transfer the filling into the prepared pie shell.

Top it with crumble.

Bake the pie for 15 minutes, then reduce the heat to 375 degrees and finish baking for another 20 to 25 minutes or until the filling is bubbling and the crumble is golden brown.

Let the pie cool for 2 hours.

Serve room temperature.

## INGREDIENTS

### FILLING

7 to 8 medium fresh peaches

4 to 5 stalks fresh rhubarb

1 cup unrefined sugar

¼ cup cornstarch

1 teaspoon vanilla

¼ teaspoon cloves

¾ teaspoon sea salt

Juice and zest of 1 lemon

5 tablespoons water + more to adjust

## TOOLS YOU'LL NEED

Cutting board

Knife

Measuring cups and spoons

Microplane grater

Saucepan

Large wooden spoon

# LAURA'S BLUEBERRY PIE

Makes one 9-inch pie

Her favorite pie for a special day. My father handpicked the blueberries and drove them to us. We passed the time picking out stems and rinsing them as the heat set in. It was worth it.

You will need: 1 double 9-inch pie crust, prepared as described on page 98.

Preheat the oven to 425 degrees.

Rinse the berries.

Let them dry.

Hold back one cup of fresh berries, combine all other filling ingredients in the saucepan.

Bring the mixture to a boil, stirring frequently with the wooden spoon.

If the filling is searing, add slightly more water.

Turn down the heat and continue cooking and stirring until the mixture is thick.

Let cool.

Fold in the remaining cup of berries.

Pour the cooled filling into the prepared bottom crust.

Top the pie, fluting or forking the edges, decorating with rolled-out scraps as desired, and applying egg wash and coarse sugar as described on page 95.

Bake the pie as described in Double-Crust Baking (page 98).

Let it cool for 2 hours.

Serve room temperature or chilled.

## INGREDIENTS

### FILLING

7 cups fresh blueberries

½ cup unrefined sugar

¼ cup brown sugar

¼ cup cornstarch

1 teaspoon vanilla

¼ teaspoon nutmeg

¼ teaspoon ginger

¾ teaspoon salt

Juice and zest of 1 lemon

5 tablespoons water + more to adjust

## TOOLS YOU'LL NEED

Measuring cups and spoons

Colander

Microplane grater

Saucepan

Large wooden spoon

# JASON'S CORNMEAL CHESS

Makes one 9-inch pie

Southern, traditional, and dependable, just like the newly wedded Jason. You want this pie in your repertoire. A friendly note: overbaking will crack the surface of the pie. The filling may jiggle when you take it out of the oven, but it will continue to bake as it sits.

You will need: 1 single 9-inch cornmeal pie crust, blind-baked (page 97).

Preheat the oven to 375 degrees.

Combine the cornmeal and flour in a medium bowl with deep sides. Set it aside.

In a separate medium bowl, whisk together the wet ingredients.

Fold the wet mix into the dry in thirds, using a large wooden spoon.

Pour the filling into the prepared pie shell.

Bake for 35 to 40 minutes.

The pie is finished when the middle is golden brown, but still jiggly.

Allow it to cool for 2 hours.

Serve room temp or chilled.

## INGREDIENTS

### FILLING

3 tablespoons cornmeal

1 tablespoon pastry flour (low protein)

4 large eggs, room temperature

1 cup buttermilk, room temperature

¼ cup sour cream, room temperature

½ cup unrefined sugar

6 tablespoons butter, melted and cooled

1 teaspoon vanilla

Zest of 1 lemon

## TOOLS YOU'LL NEED

Measuring cups and spoons

Microplane grater

2 medium-size mixing bowls with deep sides

Whisk

Large wooden spoon

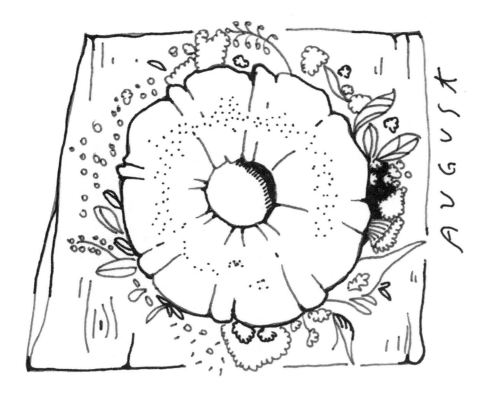

AUGUST

*When you lean in to kiss, do you pull out a manual?*
*— posted August 3*

Usually it's hot and humid in August, but this year turned particularly dry. The garden withered and wilted. I kept the herbs alive with morning and evening pails of water, performing elaborate rain dances nightly to an old weather radio. The rains, when they happened, came in sideways. Downpours that washed away all the topsoil and flooded the creek. Slouching on the front porch with my shoes off, I ate ice cream out of the carton to a purple sky shredding open.

To get anything done, I rose before the sun and slept off the early afternoon, returning to work in the evening. There's no sense in caring about how you look or what you smell like in August—you're constantly dirty. Clothes stick to your sweaty body no matter what. The poison ivy, which is everywhere around the bakery, turns vicious. After an afternoon of gathering sticks and twigs for oven kindling, my entire arm was covered in boils and blisters. Five long days of torturous itching landed me at the doctor's for a shot of steroids to reduce the rash. Lips sunburned, hair knotted, I lay on the cool, plastic seat in the air-conditioned office, haggard. August is the height of the Ferris wheel. The ride pauses for one brief look around. Is it what you imagined?

The bakery handles the heat about as well as I do. The whole place groans. The doorways and windows swell and stick. The walk-in cooler constantly needs to be defrosted. The walls must be routinely scrubbed to discourage mold. The ants show up, then the spiders. The carpenter bees arrive, drilling holes in the wooden beams alongside the oven, and the woodpeckers descend, tunneling into the beams and leaving shredded wood everywhere. More than once, a bird flies into the front window, smashing the glass. And then, lastly, the flies start hatching.

Making a decent pie crust anytime after lunch is impossible. Even if all the ingredients are frozen to start with, the pie dough will fuse to the table within minutes of rolling. Working with a sense of urgency is crucial. Too hot for anything heavy, I eat lunch by the oven under the shade. A few wooden boards piled high with toasted bread, cheese, sardines, olives, boiled eggs, grapes, pickles, jams, chickpea spread, nuts, mustard, and salt and pepper. Washing it down with chilled white wine. These moments almost make up for the humidity.

Finding a collection of old Bundt pans at a yard sale, I became obsessed with making cakes. In August, the groomsman passed through town again. This time I wasn't folding custard into pie shells; I was sifting flours and greasing old pans with lard. One night we took a drive on the back roads, eventually stopping at the grocery store for a bag of sugar and a jug of milk. Pulling into the driveway, I cut the engine off, and we sat in the dark for several minutes listening to Bruce Springsteen. The air was low and gauzy. The sky a vat of indigo. One by one, the stars punched holes in density.

A bead of sweat ran between my dress and my back. I started yammering under the blanket of warm air and the lubrication of gin: *It's just that I've given up on finding love. And I know that sounds sad, but it's not. I'm free from all the waiting and wanting and hoping.* He lit a cigarette and took a long drag, the cherry lighting up his face. *So what do you hope for?* he asked. I pressed my face into the steering wheel and looked at him sideways: *I just want to make a good cake.*

# CAKE FLOUR

Makes 3½ cups cake flour

Cake flour is low enough in protein that it will quickly hydrate into a batter without much mixing, but also strong enough that it will lift properly to ensure even baking and a moist, light interior. All-purpose flour (a 50/50 blend of pastry and bread flour) typically has a protein content between 10 and 11 percent. Cake flour, in contrast, has a lower protein content—between 8 and 9 percent. Make your own cake flour! The results are feathery light, highly moist, and very tender. I use a blend of Carolina Ground type 75 pastry flour and type 75 bread flour with Bob's Red Mill cornstarch. The cornstarch lowers the overall protein and inhibits gluten development.

Toss together the flours and cornstarch in the medium bowl.

Sift the mixture twice, or until it is thoroughly combined.

Transfer the cake flour into an airtight storage container.

Keep it in a cool and dry place.

Use as needed.

**INGREDIENTS**

1½ cups bread flour

1½ cups pastry flour (low protein)

½ cup cornstarch

**TOOLS YOU'LL NEED**

Measuring cups

Medium-size mixing bowl

Flour sifter

Airtight storage container

# EVERYDAY CAKES

As you get familiar with these recipes, you'll notice that there is one basic set of dry ingredients and a set of wet ingredients— it's the little variations that make the cake unique (I've indicated these with + signs). Don't hesitate to make your own changes to the basic recipe to create your own cakes. Read all the recipes thoroughly before beginning.

# GROOMSMAN CAKE

Makes 1 Bundt cake

He left a bottle of bourbon on the mantel. I poured it into a cake batter, baked it, and sent it to him in the mail. I don't mind being forward the old-fashioned way.

Grease the Bundt pan with butter. Dust it with flour and shake out any loose flour left. Set it aside.

Center a rack in the oven and preheat it to 350 degrees.

In a medium bowl, sift together the cake flour, baking powder, and salt.

In a separate medium bowl, sift together the sugars.

Add the butter to the sugar.

Cream together with a hand blender till light and fluffy.

Scrape down the sides of the bowl.

Add the eggs to the creamed mix one at a time, fully blending after each addition.

Scrape down the sides of the bowl.

To the creamed mixture add the milk, vanilla, and bourbon. Beat well.

Pour the wet mix into the dry mix in thirds.

Fold gently until there is no visible flour and no lumps remain in the batter.

Pour the batter into the waiting Bundt pan.

Bake in the center of the oven for 35 to 40 minutes or until a knife comes out clean.

Let the cake cool for 10 minutes.

Run a thin knife between the cake and the pan.

Flip it over onto a wire rack and cool completely.

Serve dusted with confectioners' sugar.

## INGREDIENTS

**DRY**

3 cups cake flour (page 113)

4½ teaspoons baking powder

¾ teaspoon salt

**WET**

1 cup unrefined sugar

½ cup brown sugar

¾ cup (1½ sticks) unsalted butter, room temperature

3 eggs, room temperature

1 cup whole milk, room temperature

1 teaspoon vanilla

3 tablespoons bourbon

Confectioners' sugar for dusting

## TOOLS YOU'LL NEED

Measuring cups and spoons

Standard Bundt pan (12 cups / 10 by 3½ inches)

Room-temperature butter and flour for the pan

2 medium-size mixing bowls

Flour sifter

Hand blender

Large wooden spoon

Knife

Wire rack

# SHOOTING STAR CAKE

Makes 1 Bundt cake

Herbaceous and sweet, this Bundt calls for thyme and fresh berries.

Grease the Bundt pan with butter. Dust it with flour and shake out any loose flour left. Set it aside.

Center a rack in the oven and preheat it to 350 degrees.

In a medium bowl, sift together the flour, baking powder, salt; toss in the lemon zest and thyme; mix well.

In a separate medium bowl, sift together the sugars.

Add the butter to the sugar.

Cream together with a hand blender till light and fluffy.

Scrape down the sides of the bowl.

Add the eggs to the creamed mix one at a time, fully blending after each addition.

Scrape down the sides of the bowl.

To the creamed mixture add the milk and vanilla. Beat well.

Pour the wet mix into the dry mix in thirds.

Fold gently until there is no visible flour and no lumps in the batter.

Fold in the berries.

Pour the batter into the waiting Bundt pan.

Bake the cake in the center of the oven for 35 to 40 minutes or until a knife comes out clean.

Let it cool for 10 minutes.

Run a thin knife between the cake and the pan.

Flip it over onto a wire rack and cool completely.

## INGREDIENTS

### DRY

3 cups cake flour (page 113)

4½ teaspoons baking powder

¾ teaspoon salt

Zest of 1 lemon

1 tablespoon freshly chopped thyme

### WET

1 cup sugar

½ cup brown sugar

⅔ cup unsalted butter, room temperature

3 eggs, room temperature

1 cup whole milk, room temperature

1 teaspoon vanilla

1 cup rinsed, fresh blueberries

1 cup rinsed, fresh blackberries

## TOOLS YOU'LL NEED

Measuring cups and spoons

Colander

Microplane grater

Standard Bundt pan (12 cups / 10 by 3½ inches)

Room-temperature butter and flour for the pan

2 medium-size mixing bowls

Flour sifter

Hand blender

Large wooden spoon

Knife

Wire rack

# COALFIELD CAKE

Makes 1 Bundt cake

I asked him to point to his town on a map. I looked at the snaking highway through the mountains. *Where is that?* I asked. *Deep in a coalfield,* he said.

Grease the Bundt pan with butter. Dust it with flour and shake out any loose flour left. Set it aside.

Center a rack in the oven and preheat it to 350 degrees.

In a medium bowl, sift together the flour, baking powder, salt, and cocoa powder; stir in the sage and orange zest. Set the bowl aside.

Roughly chop the chocolate.

Fill the bottom of the saucepan with water. Set it atop the cooking range.

Place the stainless-steel bowl on the saucepan.

Bring the water in the pan to a rolling boil, heating the bowl.

Toss the chocolate into the hot bowl, reduce the heat, and whisk evenly until the chocolate melts.

Carefully remove the bowl from the saucepan and let the chocolate cool.

In another medium bowl, sift together the sugars.

Add the butter to the sugar.

Cream together with a hand blender till the mixture is light and fluffy.

Scrape down the sides of the bowl.

Add the eggs to the creamed mix one at a time, fully blending after each addition.

Scrape down the sides of the bowl.

To the creamed mixture add the milk, vanilla, and sour cream.

Beat well.

## INGREDIENTS

**DRY**

$1/3$ cups cake flour (page 113)

$4\frac{1}{2}$ teaspoons baking powder

$3/4$ teaspoon salt

$1/2$ cup unsweetened cocoa powder

2 tablespoons chopped sage

Zest of 1 orange

**WET**

5 ounces 60% cacao baking chocolate

1 cup unrefined sugar

$1/2$ cup brown sugar

$2/3$ cup unsalted butter, room temperature

3 eggs, room temperature

1 cup whole milk, room temperature

1 teaspoon vanilla

$1/2$ cup sour cream

Ganache glaze (recipe on page 123)

## TOOLS YOU'LL NEED

Measuring cups and spoons

Microplane grater

Standard Bundt pan (12 cups / 10 by $3\frac{1}{2}$ inches)

Room-temperature butter and flour, for the pan

2 medium-size mixing bowls

Flour sifter

Add the cooled, melted chocolate.

Beat well.

Pour the wet mix into the dry mix in thirds.

Fold gently until there is no visible flour and no lumps in the batter.

Pour the batter into the waiting pan.

Bake the cake in the center of the oven for 35 to 40 minutes or until a thin knife comes out clean.

Let it cool for 10 minutes.

Run a thin knife between the cake and the pan.

Flip it over onto a wire rack.

Cool completely.

Pour the ganache glaze over the cooled cake.

Chopping knife

Cutting board

Digital scale

Saucepan

Medium-size stainless-steel bowl

Whisk

Hand blender

Large wooden spoon

Thin-blade knife

Wire rack

# GRATEFUL GANACHE GLAZE

Roughly chop the chocolate.

Fill the bottom of the saucepan with water. Set it atop the cooking range.

Place the stainless-steel bowl on top of the saucepan.

Bring the water in the pan to a rolling boil, heating the bowl.

Toss the chocolate into the hot bowl, reduce the heat, and whisk evenly until the chocolate melts.

Carefully remove the bowl from the saucepan.

While whisking, drizzle in a third of the heavy cream.

Whisk till combined.

Drizzle in another third.

Whisk to combine.

Drizzle in the remaining heavy cream and whisk thoroughly.

Pour the ganache over a cooled cake.

## TIPS

Setting the cake on a wire rack in a sheet tray makes for easy cleanup. Since this glaze is only two ingredients, don't skimp on the quality. If you want a thinner ganache, drizzle in more heavy cream. If you want a thicker, more frosting-like ganache, reduce the heavy cream. Ganache works best when applied over a chilled cake—if the surface is still hot, it will slide right off.

**INGREDIENTS**

8 ounces bittersweet baking chocolate, at least 60% cacao

1 cup heavy cream

**TOOLS YOU'LL NEED**

Digital scale

Chopping knife

Cutting board

Saucepan

Medium, deep, stainless-steel bowl

Whisk

Potholders

Measuring cup

# JOSEPHINE'S WHIPPED CREAM

Makes enough to cover a pie or a few dollops per slice of cake.

Place the bowl and all whisks in the freezer for 10 minutes.

Pour the cold heavy cream into the chilled bowl.

Beat with the hand blender till soft peaks form. Sift in the confectioners' sugar and drizzle in the maple syrup.

Add the orange zest.

Beat with the hand blender for about 5 more seconds.

Set the hand blender aside and finish whipping with a hand whisk.

### INGREDIENTS

1 cup heavy cream, chilled

2 tablespoons confectioners' sugar

2 tablespoons maple syrup

Zest of 1 orange

### TOOLS YOU'LL NEED

Measuring cup and spoons

Microplane grater

Flour sifter

Deep metal bowl

Hand blender

Whisk

SEPTEMBER

I have baked all the apples I
have for you.
— posted september 21

I went to town to buy a good axe, a wheel of cheese, and a
bushel of apples. The market stalls told a tale of summer
kissing fall. Tomatoes, peppers, peaches, grapes, winter
squash, kale, and the first flush of apples. The heat faded, coming
to call only in the afternoon, and the light took on a sideways slant.

Every year my Northern blood curses summer in the South, and every fall there is no other place I'd rather be. Yellows and reds wave from the tree branches. Goldenrod and aster sing from the pastures. I see a leaf fall: my heart gets caught in my throat. How many times have we wished someone would leave, only to miss them as soon as the door closes?

Preparations for winter ensued. On a breezy, blue afternoon, I harvested the winter squash that managed to survive the drought and whatever apples I could get from the tree next to the pond. Loads of slab wood for the bakery and cordwood for the house arrived. I spent the following days splitting and stacking with friends. Cordwood that wouldn't fit in the woodshed was piled on the porch. In the morning, with hot coffee in hand, I stepped out like the captain of a ship to meet a bank of fog. My spirit came back after being expelled through heat and exhaustion. I could feel my skin again, no longer an oil slick of soot and sweat. I welcomed the brush of wool and silk.

The farmer who raises cattle in the neighborhood also keeps a field of tobacco down the road. When the first flowers appear on the plants, they "sucker" them, cutting off the blossoms to direct energy toward the leaves. The tobacco plant in maturity is a beautiful sight. Five feet tall, give or take, with broad leaves radiating from a single stalk. When the time is right, somewhere in the first week or two of the month, the plants get slashed and staked to dry before being piled in baskets and taken away in truck beds. In the summer, Laura and I sneak out into the field to be dwarfed by the plants. In September, we sneak out to see the leaves spread like dancers' skirts, turning yellow.

The practice of baking now begs for a little more embellishment. Bread doughs behave in temperatures they adore. Pie crust doesn't threaten to bake just resting on the workbench. I slow down and turn to the fine details. In a time when a bag of chips can be labeled "artisanal," I find it essential to give some integrity back

to the word. Artisans are meant to transform themselves through their work. You cannot look like an artisan. You cannot even be an artisan. The artisanal path is an invisible process deep inside the wild darkness of your chest. The journey is never done and yet is always attempted. Growth and change are inevitable.

September 21: the last day of summer. Over a few beers on the porch, Laura, Jason, and I decided to get on the river in search of pawpaws. We'd found them a month ago. The water was high then, right after a downpour. Maneuvering our canoes through a tricky side passage to the left of an island with no name, we had to lie down in the boat to pass under fallen tree trunks. Looking up at a matrix of branches, I saw them: huge clusters of neon green pawpaws simultaneously in plain sight and completely hidden.

One last rumble. One last truck careening down a dirt road. One last shot at playing hooky. Driving the road next to the river, trying to jog our memories, we took an educated guess and parked in a turnoff, dragging the canoe through the trees down to the water. The three of us ferried across in the wide red canoe. Shored the boat, bushwhacked across the island, and surprisingly, arrived at the exact same spot we had been a month ago. There was nothing. The pawpaw trees were beautiful. And completely barren. In it for the adventure and impressed enough with our navigational skills, we weren't entirely downtrodden. But then something else kicked in. A disbelief. A rejection of the obvious. We split apart to see if we could find some evidence. A rotten pawpaw was better than none at all.

Sandals crunching on dried leaves. Unidentifiable shrubs and branches up my skirt. Bugs in my ear. I felt childish. A signature of adulthood is accepting disappointment gracefully, but all I wanted to do was pout. Next time we could get our hands on them was a year away, and who knew if we'd ever get back to this spot? Just one more step. Just one more look. Just a few more minutes. And then, when I spotted a fallen one nestled in a pile of leaves, I felt childish in another way: unbridled, selfish, and saturated with enthusiasm. I screamed. And then Jason screamed. We hit a hot spot, shaking the trees and raking the ground. I frantically gathered handfuls in my skirt, jumping up and down. The whole world was raining tiny green treasures.

The pawpaw, a huge berry, is the largest edible fruit native to North America. Preferring semishade and thicket, pawpaws are often choked out of well-established forests. They do well along rivers and bottomland, ranging from the Gulf Coast up to the Great Lakes. Forming in clusters of two to five fruits, pawpaws on the same tree can ripen at different times, so if you find a patch, it's worthwhile to visit several times. They bruise easily, the major reason they've been left behind in the gross industrialization of agriculture. Once removed from their environment, they need to be eaten within two to three days. Looking down at the one in my hand, I could almost watch it turn from green to brown.

A bitter taste and a pear-like consistency at first—the skin was thin, scraping it away with my teeth revealed a banana-like, custardy interior studded with several large black seeds. I bit again, this time taking in a mouthful and eating it like a watermelon, spitting the seeds aside. Good art makes you uncomfortable. The flavor of the pawpaw is like that, a wave of tropical delights: pineapple, mango, banana, and then a musky flavor that leaves a question mark on your tongue. Hard to tell what I was tasting. I bit again and again, till it was gone. Juice dripped down my chin, my humanity restored.

# AWE PAWPAW PIE

Makes one 9-inch pie

Just like we stripped away the germ from the wheat, we've stripped away the wild element of life and, while stabilizing it, left it with little flavor. Go out and hunt for your pie. It will taste better. Enjoy this pie the same day it's baked for best results. Remove the "meat" from the pawpaw by peeling away the skin (fingers work fine) and scraping the interior away from the seeds.

You will need: 1 single 9-inch pie crust, blind-baked (page 97) whipped cream for serving (page 125)

Preheat the oven to 375 degrees.

Combine all the filling ingredients in a blender and puree.

Pour the filling into the prepared pie shell.

Bake for 35 minutes or until golden brown on the edges and slightly jiggly in the center.

Let the pie cool for 2 hours.

Refrigerate.

Serve chilled with whipped cream.

## INGREDIENTS

### FILLING

1¼ cups pawpaw fruit

4 eggs

1 cup unrefined sugar

1 cup whole milk, room temperature

4 tablespoons (½ stick) melted and cooled butter

1 teaspoon vanilla

¼ teaspoon nutmeg

¼ teaspoon salt

### TOOLS YOU'LL NEED

Measuring cups and spoons

Small saucepan

Blender

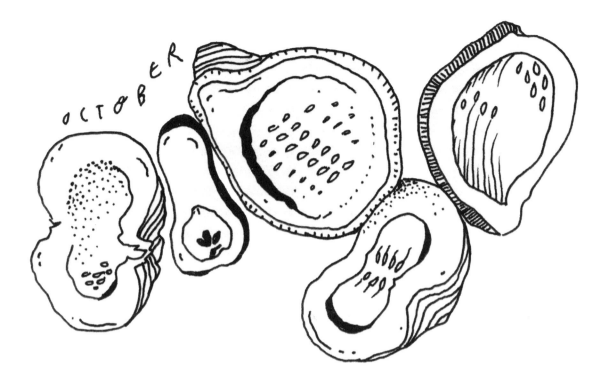

OCTOBER

*It's the ephemeral details that turn the ordinary to the devotional.*
— *posted october 15*

I woke up twisted in a tsunami of anger. Soaked sheets. Blinds askew. The living room light still on. Peeling back bedding and kicking pillows to the floor, I coasted past my shoes, grabbing a knife and several squash, and made a barefoot beeline for the picnic tables. Animosity must be expelled from the body in a constructive form. Piercing the flesh, driving the knife deep into cavity of a giant blue hubbard, I heard a tearing pop. Prying the shell open, boring my fingers into the stringy hollows, gouging out the seeds like the eyes of my enemy. Hacking, chopping, and exhausted. My insides on the out. Sometimes the hurt comes from nowhere.

There are as many different flavors of loneliness as there are varieties of winter squash. On a rainy day in October, I feel as if I've tasted them all. Loneliness is a multidimensional experience: striking my chest in the thick of a crowd or lying in the fading grass alone. It is my biggest teacher and my lifelong friend. It is not the job of love to cure loneliness. Learn how to be lonely. I believe it is our hope for the future. The more we can be at rest with ourselves, the less harm we do grasping for distraction.

So please, put down your phone. Our wholeness, our tenderness, the subtle marks of time, cannot be mitigated by screens, algorithms, and notifications. Having a wealth of information about someone is not the same as knowing them. Knowing someone is knowing the story they will tell at every party. Knowing someone is being able to pick out their laughter from the next room. Knowing someone is knowing at what point in the movie they fall asleep. While around us is a whirlwind of numbers and codes, between us is a calm current. We are living in unprecedented times. We are unprecedented lovers.

The onslaught of technologies that claim to make us visible has turned us into apparitions wandering long corridors between the courtship rituals of the past and futuristic dial-up dates. In a new land with no rules, I find myself turning toward tradition for comfort. While the ability and means to express ourselves has proliferated, we lack the skills to decipher the flood of signals we receive. What are you telling me? What am I to do? The phone crackles and breaks. I see you saw my message and never responded. I see a green blinking light. I know you're out there.

Our inability to sit with discomfort has damaged our sense of empathy. In the end, what hurt so much about losing my farmer was not that the love withered or even that he loved another, but that he couldn't say it to my face. But we don't get answers. And it's better not to just make them up. We must go on. Bereft in the wreckage, I saw that before we left each other: I left myself. I left when I put the responsibility for my happiness in someone

else's hands. I left when I was uncomfortable, but never spoke up because I was afraid to be alone. I left when I turned the rage inward, hurting no one but myself. By the time he started packing his bags, I was already a ghost wandering the halls.

Return to the mixing bowl. The pie tin. The rolling pin. Sit with yourself. It will all come up. Let it. In the heart of life lives a profound tenderness. A longing that penetrates every pore of our material body. You cannot fill it with another person or food. It is designed to be eternally open. It is our path back to the source. Learn how to struggle against the need to constantly be doing, to be seen, to be plugged in. Remain in the present moment. Love is a force of nature. We have as much control over it as we do the tide of the ocean. The best chance we have in absorbing its awesome power is to stay open. Love is trying to find a way into the world: be a conduit.

What I have left now to love of you is your memory, and it pours from the stinking, split-open squash. I turn my face to a wavy recollection. I hold out my hand. Slanted beams of sunlight filter through wavering branches. Light ripples. Look, here, into my eyes. I want to see you. Let me see how time has graced a wrinkle next to your eye or one right by your lip where you smile so much. Let me see the dirt under your nails and how long your hair has grown. And now go and let me be in peace.

## HOW TO TAKE A DEEP BREATH

Our breath is a self-healing mechanism. Find a comfortable place to relax for a few minutes. Stand with your hands hanging by your sides, your feet firmly planted on the ground, and your chin slightly tilted upward. Breathe normally for several breaths. Begin to notice the breath moving through your body. Remember that the breath floods the back of the body, not just the chest and stomach. Take a breath deep in through your nose to your belly to the count of four, pause, exhale from the belly out through the nose to the count of four. As you breathe in, hold this in your mind: *I am breathing in calm and peace.* As you breathe out, focus on the opposite: *I am breathing out tension and anxiety.* Repeat as needed.

# GHOST PIE

Makes one 9-inch pie

Honor the dead by living.

You'll need: 1 single 9-inch pie crust, blind-baked (page 97), coarse sugar for dusting, whipped cream for serving (page 125)

Preheat the oven to 400 degrees.

Quarter the squashes. Lay them pulp side down on a sheet pan, pierce them with a fork, and bake for 1 hour or until tender.

Let them cool.

Scoop the squash into the medium bowl.

Mash and measure out 2 cups (saving any extra for another use).

In a food processor, combine the softened butter and sugars.

Cream.

With the food processor running, add the eggs, one at a time.

Now, add in the coconut cream, sorghum syrup, cinnamon, ginger, cloves, and salt.

Last, add the mashed squash and blend until fully incorporated.

Pour the filling into the prepared pie shell.

Dust with coarse sugar.

Bake for 30 to 35 minutes or until the top is golden brown and the center is a little jiggly.

Let the pie cool for 2 hours.

Serve room temp or chilled with whipped cream.

## INGREDIENTS

2 large butternut squashes (or about 2 to 2½ pounds other winter squash such as pumpkin, blue hubbard, or Cinderella)

4 tablespoons (½ stick) unsalted butter, room temperature

⅓ cup unrefined sugar

⅓ cup brown sugar

3 eggs, room temperature

¼ cup coconut cream, room temperature

1 tablespoon sorghum syrup

¼ teaspoon cinnamon

¼ teaspoon ginger

¼ teaspoon cloves

¼ teaspoon salt

## TOOLS YOU'LL NEED

Measuring cups and spoons

Sheet pan

Fork

Large wooden spoon

Medium-size mixing bowl

Food processor

# LONELY BIRD PIE

Makes one 9-inch pie

Lonely is a state of mind. Prepare the blind-baked crust and egg wash while the sweet potatoes are roasting.

You will need: 1 single 9-inch cornmeal pie crust, blind-baked (page 97), Coarse sugar for dusting

Preheat the oven to 400 degrees.

Poke the sweet potatoes several times with the tines of a fork.

Bake them for 1 hour on a parchment-lined sheet pan.

When they are tender if pressed with a fork, remove them from the oven.

Let cool; keep the oven at 400 degrees.

Peel and mash the sweet potatoes.

Measure out 3 cups of the mashed sweet potatoes, saving the rest for a snack.

In a food processor, combine the butter and sugar, and blend till smooth.

With the food processor on, add the eggs, one at a time.

To this, add the sweet potato mash, coconut milk, and vanilla.

Add the cinnamon, nutmeg, and salt.

Blend till the filling is creamy and smooth.

Pour it into the prepared pie crust.

Dust with coarse sugar.

Bake for 30 to 35 minutes at 400 degrees or until the filling is set with a slight jiggle to the center.

Let the pie cool for 2 hours.

Serve room temperature or chilled.

## INGREDIENTS

4 to 5 medium-size sweet potatoes

4 tablespoons (½ stick) unsalted butter, softened

⅓ cup unrefined sugar

⅓ cup coconut milk

1 teaspoon vanilla

3 eggs, room temperature

¼ teaspoon cinnamon

¼ teaspoon nutmeg

¼ teaspoon salt

## TOOLS YOU'LL NEED

Measuring cups and spoons

Fork

Sheet pan

Parchment paper

Large wooden spoon

Food processor

NOVEMBER

Does this count as skin to skin contact?
— posted NOVEMBER 20

It seemed that attending weddings would be our way of bonding, the groomsman and me. We met under falling leaves at Hungry Mother State Park in Virginia to watch Matt and Sarah tie the knot. Separated by state borders, bakery work, and grad school, these adventurous weekends together pumped fresh air into our lungs, rekindling an undeniable attraction. I was on the verge of letting my hands off the handlebars, but unlike falling in love in my twenties, I now wanted to know the important details first, preferring not to wake up in three years and find out he was never looking for anything long-term and hated eggs sunny side up. I once told a friend that I had only three questions I wanted to ask a man. Now was my chance to walk the talk.

Caravanning up the mountains the day before with Laura and Jason, we staked our claim, scavenged for firewood, cracked open a few beers, and dusted off the picnic tables. I made a bed fit for a shepherd in the back of my car out of a ragtag assortment of pillows, blankets, and sleeping bags. Well past dark, his face emerged from behind a cloud of campfire smoke covered in a woolly beard and a beaming smile. Damn those twinkling eyes.

The first question seemed casual enough, given our circumstances. As we rinsed our toothbrushes under a water spigot, I asked him if he believed in marriage. "Yeah," he said, "I do." He was known for his penchant toward revolutionary politics; his friends had warned me that if I was looking for something traditional, I should run the other way. I reeled back and spit out a stream of foamy mint-flavored toothpaste. I was shocked by his confidence and even further surprised by how important this question was to me.

I realized that although I had hoped to marry almost every single person I'd dated, in all my years I'd never actually asked anyone their feelings point-blank, preferring to play it cool. The whistle on the kettle blew. One down, two to go.

Arranged in a park shelter covered in pine needles and held up by lumbering beams, attendees brought homemade pies to compete in a friendly yet ruthless contest. Perfectly placed tablecloths, Ball jars, slips of paper, pens, and handwritten signs marked the categories on the various tables. Laura and I registered our pies, and I left mine in the apple section, moving on to examine the awards, which included a blender from the seventies and a mobile made from whisks.

I had made a completely burned deep-dish apple pie to enter into the fruit category. Baked in a 9-inch springform pan, it was heavy on the crust, with enough filling for two pies. I broiled the pie while packing my bags and, of course, blackened the entire top. I've got a thing for the ugly duckling, so I tucked it in a basket covered in a linen shroud, hoping that by the time we got to the party, it would have molted into a swan. Snatching it from the passenger seat where it survived the trip, I noticed that it left a deep, dark, circular stain of melted butter: a memory of the weekend already fused into fabric.

*The rules:* To vote for a pie in category, you must taste all the pies listed in that category. You may vote in as many categories as you like, one vote per category. Lobbying is encouraged. You may make up a new category—perhaps one that applies only to your pie?

Nothing about it was fair. Everything about it was fun. After a merry-go-ground of sweet pies, savory pies, pudding pies, chocolate pies, fruit pies, tomato pies, and slab pies, the winners were announced. The groomsman leaned in: *I have to tell you something you're not going to like,* he said. I cocked my eyebrow: *Oh, really?*

*Yeah,* he said, *I voted against you in one category: the prettiest pie.* The corner of my mouth twitched down. *Which one did you prefer?* He looked me square in the eye: *I liked the one with hearts all over it.*

The campground bordered a lake and provided boat rentals, so we headed down to the water to work off our gluttony. Prepared only for mischief, we cobbled together the fee, stripped down to our underwear, and hopped on a metallic blue paddleboat, with his dog riding on top of life jackets wedged between us. Pedaling far from shore and down past the beaches and water slides, we jumped off and swam, watching each other's faces underwater in slow motion. Fallen trees on the edge cast bony shadows. Wrapped up in a beach towel, raking my fingertips through tangled hair, I asked him if he wanted to have children. *Yes,* he said, *definitely.* Just then, we felt the bump of a yellow canoe: it was Laura and Jason. Time to get our fancy clothes on.

Zipping zippers, buckling belts, and lacing knots in the back of our cars and tents. Using rearview mirrors and the surface of the tin coffeepot, we checked our teeth and applied powder and gloss. We cleaned up as best we could, stopping here and there for a swig of bourbon. We had all packed dark green and blue clothes, and he needed to differentiate somehow. Ripping apart the collar of an old red shirt, he tucked it in his vest and offered me a strand to wear as a bracelet. I did so proudly.

The ceremony was brief and beautiful. The flower girl, rather than tossing the flowers evenly, grabbed them by the fistful and placed them in clumps along the path. I understood. When something is so beautiful and good, you want to take it by the handful. A ritual filled with pledges, rings, and prayers under a fall arbor. I could tell, on some level, we wondered if we'd ever be standing together in the same way.

Avoiding the dinner line, we ran off to the island that was visible from the lodge. It was homecoming, and the place was flooded with teenagers and their families taking pictures. We looked like a bunch of hippies cutting through a drag ball. And we kind of were. I made sure to tell each girl we passed how pretty she looked. They were like deer in headlights— you could almost smell an anxious, hormonal perfume in the twilight breeze. I was equally terrified and thrilled for them. Crossing the boardwalk to the island, he took my hand, leading me down a soft path till we came to an amphitheater with long plank benches, lights, and a little stage. Sitting on the edge of the platform, in the last glimpse of sunlight, I asked him if he believed in God. He responded in a low, steady voice that made my whole body flush. "You?" he asked. A tear welled up in the corner of my eye. I opened my mouth. A twig cracked in the distance, and a jumble of shouting partygoers erupted into the scene. Our friends called to us from across the water to come eat.

The first ring of dancers poured cornmeal on the concrete floor and scuffled it in while they promenaded and swung their neighbors. I had never, in my life, danced with a partner. I liked to do my own thing and move around wherever I wanted. That was, perhaps, my whole way of living at this point. He had never done it either, but before we had fallen asleep the night before, we'd promised to give it a try. Getting into a square, we waved to the band, shot the owl, bowed to our partners, ripped the snark, wove the basket, and squared the set. We messed up, tried again, and laughed with our heads back to a room of stomping feet, kicked-up skirts, and clapping hands. Slowing it down for a two-step, we fused together and bumped our way around in an awkward circle, getting it right for a while and then losing it. I pressed my lips to his ear: *It works best when we're not thinking about it.*

The next day, Laura, Jason, the groomsman, and I broke off to camp in the coalfields. Rising up on a high pass, I saw a strip mine for the first time. It hit my chest like a ton of bricks. A giant swath of mountainside torn away to get at bands of coal streaked through the bedrock like frosting in a layer cake. Peeling out into an overlook, we spilled out of our cars to behold the stunning and dismantled landscape. My eyes refocused and adjusted continually, straining to comprehend what unfurled before us. It was like the first time I saw a clear-cut. No words and a million questions simultaneously swamped my mind. A steady drone of machinery in the background sang a chilling lullaby. We stood sobered. Across the highway hid a washed-out dirt road that led to an old resort, now used as an event space. Retreating into the thicket, we sought refuge.

We set camp in a sandpit under a sign hanging by one nail that read MARS ROCKS: CLIMB AT YOUR OWN RISK and pulled together a meal of beans and rice along with foraged mushrooms. Donning winter jackets and hats to guard against the settling frost, we traipsed around the hundred-acre property that included a graveyard for broken refrigerators, several haunted cabins, and a boathouse on a pond that desperately needed water. Climbing up to the flats, a stretch of land that housed a stage, a pavilion, and an assortment of Airstream trailers in different stages of decomposition, the view opened. We could make out the backbone of Appalachia, just barely visible under the toenail moon. With our breath full of whiskey, we wondered what would become of this place, how the economy was going to rejuvenate itself, and what kind of world we wanted for our hypothetical children.

Warming by the late-night fire, polishing off leftover chunks of apple pie, the owls called. The starts shot back and forth in a game of cosmic pinball. Laura and Jason wandered off to bed, and we remained, wrapped in quilts full of sand. He reached out his hand to me, and high above equipment breaking open the heart of the world, above weedy strips of grass between the highway, above the throaty call of the last crickets, above rusted cars sinking into the torrid soil, above boarded-up storefronts, we practiced our two-step.

Quick, quick, slow, slow. Quick, quick, slow, slow.

Drunken feet scuffling the dirt into tiny clouds, counting and concentrating until we gave in and just held on to each other, swaying and teetering. We would dance on our own graves before we let the powers that be dance on us.

# HOLD A PIE CONTEST

These are the instructions from the wedding invitation.
(Thanks, Matt and Sarah.) Make up your own!

### RULES

- Bring a pie that you bake. Or just come and eat pie.

- No canned pie filling. Canned pumpkin or fruit is
  okay, but if possible, use fresh fruit/vegetables.

- Write down your recipe and be prepared to jot down if
  it is gluten free, vegan, or other dietary restriction.

- Safety issues: Since there are only three ovens and
  refrigerators at our disposal, please try not to bring pies
  that need to be warmed, frozen, or kept cold. Let me
  know if you need space in an oven or fridge if you go this
  route. Also, no uncooked eggs; bake the meringue.

- Arrival: Please arrive on time! We have a very short window
  after the contest to get ready for the ceremony. Any delays
  will result in the wedding party not partaking in the awards.

- Everyone's a judge, whether you bake a pie or come
  to eat. You can either pick one category to judge or
  judge all the categories, but in order to cast your
  vote, you must try all the pies in that category.

- Choose a category to enter. Enter as many pies
  as you like. There will be a category for prettiest
  pie, so this category will be judged first.

### TIME FRAME

11:30 A.M. Pie registration

12:00 P.M. to 1:00 P.M. Judging begins (everyone's a judge)

1:30 P.M. to 2:00 P.M. Prizes awarded

## CATEGORIES

Fruit

Nut

Cream (shell and filling baked separately, then combined—
   e.g., lemon meringue, coconut cream, Key lime)

Custard (filling cooked in the pie—e.g., sweet potato, pumpkin, chess)

Chocolate

Heirloom (old-fashioned pie from a family recipe)

Cobblers and Crisps

Gluten Free (can enter into other categories if desired)

Savory Pies

Youth (under 18)

Beginner (first pie at any age)

Pielets (fried pies, mini tarts)

English Literature Pies (e.g., Edgar Allan Pie, Pies and Prejudice . . . )

Prettiest Pie

Most Creative Pie

Most Creative Pie Name

It Was Pretty Before It Got Here

Tasted the Most Pies

Best in Show (crust, looks, taste)


Prizes: handmade books, handmade crafts, vintage kitchen
   gadgets, aprons, jams, cookbooks, and more

# APPLE PIE

Makes one 9-inch pie

When you choose the apples for this pie, blend sweet and tart apples, as well as a mix of firm and soft varieties. I prefer working with Golden Delicious, Goldrush, Honeycrisp, Mutsu, and Pink Lady. Check your farmers' market to find out what grows well in your area.

You will need: 1 double 9-inch pie crust, prepared as described on page 98

Preheat the oven to 425 degrees.

Prepare the apples by coring and thinly slicing them, leaving the skins on.

In the large bowl, toss together the sliced apples, sugars, cornstarch, spices, and salt.

Add the lemon zest, lemon juice, and vanilla.

Toss again.

Fill the prepared bottom crust with the apple mixture, mounding it slightly higher in the center.

Cover the filling with the top crust, then crimp and finish as indicated on page 96.

Bake the pie for 10 minutes, then reduce the heat to 375.

Continue to bake for 35 to 40 minutes. When the pastry is golden brown, the filling boiling, and the fruit tender, the pie is done.

Cool for 2 hours.

Serve at room temperature or chilled.

INGREDIENTS

**FILLING**

5 to 6 medium apples

½ cup unrefined sugar

¼ cup brown sugar

¼ cup cornstarch

¼ teaspoon cinnamon

¼ teaspoon nutmeg

¼ teaspoon ginger

¾ teaspoon salt

Zest of 1 lemon

Juice of ½ lemon

1 tablespoon vanilla

TOOLS YOU'LL NEED

Measuring cups and spoons

Microplane grater

Knife

Cutting board

Large mixing bowl

# DEEP-DISH APPLE PIE

Makes one deep 9-inch pie

For this pie, you'll use two recipes' worth of double-crust apple pie crust and double the usual amount of filling as well. Due to the volume of filling, the prepared apples must be cooked down ahead of time to bake evenly.

You will need: 2 double-crust doughs, prepared ahead of time. One entire double-crust dough will be the bottom, while the other will be the top and extra for decoration. Chill in the refrigerator till the apple filling has been cooked and cooled and the oven is at temperature.

In a large pot, combine all the filling ingredients and bring the mixture to a boil.

Turn the heat down to low.

Cook, stirring with a large wooden spoon to keep the apples from burning on the bottom.

When the filling is bubbling thick and the apples are tender to the tines of a fork, it's done.

Cool the filling to room temp, stirring occasionally.

Preheat the oven to 415 degrees.

Line the bottom of the springform pan with parchment.

Spray the sides evenly with a nonstick spray.

Bring out one portion of the resting pie dough.

Roll into a large sheet.

Fold it over the rolling pin or your arm, lift, and set it into the springform pan.

## INGREDIENTS

### FILLING

10 to 11 medium and large apples, cored and thinly sliced

1½ cups unrefined sugar

½ cup brown sugar

½ cup cornstarch

2 tablespoons vanilla

½ teaspoon cinnamon

½ teaspoon nutmeg

½ teaspoon ginger

1½ teaspoons salt

Zest of 2 lemons

Juice of 1 lemon

2 to 3 cups water

2 egg yolks

2 tablespoons heavy cream

Coarse sugar for dusting

### TOOLS YOU'LL NEED

Knife

Cutting board

Measuring cups and spoons

Microplane grater

Large pot

Large wooden spoon

9-inch springform pan

Parchment paper

Nonstick cooking spray

Rolling pin

Tuck it into the bottom of the pan and press it firmly against the sides.

Trim the excess dough along the edge, leaving 1 inch all the way around.

Fill it with the cooled apple filling.

Roll the second portion of pie dough into a large sheet.

Use a 9-inch pie tin to trace a circle on the dough, leaving a ½ inch extra around the edge.

Cut.

Cover the pie with the crust.

Fold the lip of the bottom crust over the top crust and pinch around the circumference.

In a small bowl, whisk together the egg yolk and cream. Brush this egg wash onto the pie.

Dust it with coarse sugar.

Place the pie on a sheet pan lined with parchment. Bake it for 90 minutes or until it is deeply browned, with the filling slightly overflowing and/or bubbling.

Immediately after removing the pie from the oven, run a sharp knife along the edge between the pan and the crust. Let it cool for 15 minutes. Pop open the ring and carefully remove it.

Continue to cool the pie for 4 hours. Expect some settling as it cools. Just like a well-loved house or pair of shoes.

TOOLS YOU'LL NEED (CONT.)

9-inch pie tin

Small bowl

Whisk

Pastry brush

Sheet pan

# BEET PAINT

Adding color, shapes, and textures is a good way to enhance the winning qualities of a pie. Inspired by the weavers and printmakers around me, I look to barn quilts, classic knit patterns, and ancient symbols for inspiration. Art reflects the world it lives in. Look around your world and translate what you see to your design.

A paint made from beets may be used on the crust on any pie you choose to make, whether brushed freehand onto individual pieces of dough or washed over a stencil to leave an image when the stencil is removed. This mixture doesn't leave much in the way of flavor, but if applied right, it will impart a deep red or pink stain on the crust. It takes a few times to get the hang of it.

You will need: 1 double-crust pie, filled as desired, but not yet covered with the top crust

INGREDIENTS

2 medium beets

2 egg yolks

2 tablespoons water

Coarse sugar for dusting

Egg wash (1 egg yolk mixed with 1 tablespoon heavy cream), if pastry cutouts are to be placed on the pie

TOOLS YOU'LL NEED

Measuring spoons

Roasting dish with lid

Knife

Cutting board

Blender

Airtight storage container

Pastry brush

Stencil

Preheat the oven to 400 degrees. Place the beets in the roasting dish, cover, and bake for 45 minutes or until the beets are tender to the touch of a fork. Let them cool.

Peel away the skins and quarter the beets.

Place them in the blender with the eggs and water. Blend the mixture into a creamy paste. There should be no chunks of beet, and the paste should be smooth.

Store the beet paint in an airtight container. Keep it refrigerated.

Create your pie, pausing after the top crust is cut but while it is still on the table. Paint your design on freehand or, if you're stenciling, place your stencil on the dough and brush the beet paint over it. One pass is enough. Brushing too many times will cause it to seep under the stencil, leaving blurred edges instead of clean lines. Read helpful tips on making a stencil on page 71.

Lift the beet-painted top with one hand on the edge and the other supporting it underneath and center it on the pie. Fold the edges over and crimp or fork the rim. Poke it several times with the tines of a fork. Sprinkle it with dusting sugar.

If you want to attach other decorative pastry cutouts, brush their undersides with egg wash in order to secure them, but don't brush the whole top of the pie. *This method excludes egg wash over the whole top, resulting in a vivid image with a bit less gloss.*

Bake the pie as directed in the recipe.

## SHAPES

Save your scraps of pie dough and form them into a ball. Roll them out into an even ⅛-inch-thick sheet. Using a pastry wheel, cut free-form shapes from the dough. Dough can also be cut with scissors, an X-Acto knife, and cookie cutters. I began cutting shapes into dough after working in paper cuts for many years. Understanding that a cold, firm sheet of dough is akin to a large, thick piece of paper, I cut and arranged the dough in a collage. Your hand has a shape it wants to make. With enough practice, your own voice will emerge. Rolling balls of dough between your hands is very simple and pretty, too. If the balls are quite tall, flatten them a bit between your finger and thumb before decorating with them.

A note: The taller the shapes rise above the crust, the quicker they will bake and color. Personally, I enjoy the charred look and taste of the taller shapes. Just as in bread, color equals flavor, and we look for the same trinity of deep brown, rusty red, and golden yellow in our crust. Having various heights of dough at different stages of caramelization enhances the overall flavor of your crust, making design not only heartwarming, but functional. Remember that when fusing shapes together or placing them on the top of your pie, there must be egg wash underneath to hold them fast.

## TEXTURE

To add texture to your pie dough, limit yourself to a few common tools. I prefer a fork. This works best with a chilled dough. Dip your fork in a bowl of flour and press it, evenly and firmly, a quarter of the way into the dough. You can crosshatch it like the top of a peanut butter cookie, meet the edges tip to tip at an angle to create a mountain-like shape, and use the tines and the end to poke free-form patterns. Find inspiration in needlepoint, cross-stitching, and weaving images. If you plan to texture the top of your pie, do so when the top crust is still lying flat on the table. Assemble the pie after you've pricked and pressed the top.

This is how I return to myself.
— posted DECEMBER 11

In December, the icicles melt by noon, but the chill stays in the air. I bring in the long limb of a cherry tree to adorn with lights, golden baubles, and paper angels. Candles are set in the windows, and I hang my patchwork-childhood stocking behind the stove. The garden is mulched over with newspaper and hay, the leaves are raked out of the gutters, and the whole place gets a final clean before the cold settles in. I start stockpiling onions, potatoes, and bags of coffee.

Walking out to fire the oven in the evening, my breath makes cloudy sculptures in a misty fog. Breaking up the kindling and setting the lay fire, I lean against the brick and take a deep breath. Winter places a cold hand on my burning forehead: It's okay, child. It's time to rest.

I wake at two A.M. to check the progress. It's a short walk to the oven from my bed, but it's still a walk. Gathering my nightgown above my knees, I stumble barefoot over the doorstep, outside past the cordwood across from the chopping block. Next to the log bench, I halt, rubbing my eyes, in front of the fire. The ground is cold and hard against my feet. Reading the flames, I make decisions about what kind of wood and how much to add. Turning away from the pulsing orange glow, I dip out to the stacks of poplar and oak. There, between parted clouds, I can see the moon. I make a wish, the same wish I've always made on every single birthday candle, dandelion, and four-leaf clover. Maybe this time it will come true? After hefting wood into the hungry chamber, I cross my arms tightly, walking back to bed as snow starts to fall.

## LUNAR CYCLES

During a lunar month, the moon will pass through four stages: new, first quarter, full, and third quarter. A new moon occurs when the moon is between the Earth and the sun. The sun is shining light on the backside of the moon, so the surface facing the Earth remains dark. A first-quarter moon takes place between the new and full moon. Here, the moon is at a ninety-degree angle between the Earth and the sun and exactly half is lit up. A full moon arrives when the moon is again in alignment with the Earth and the Sun, but this time the sun is across from the moon. A third-quarter moon is between the full and new moon, when again, the moon finds itself at a ninety-degree angle to the Earth.

Within each of the transitional phases are terms we can use

to help understand how much of the moon's surface is visible: crescent, gibbous, waxing, and waning. When the moon is less than 50 percent illuminated, it is referred to as a crescent moon. A moon is said to be gibbous when over 50 percent is illuminated. Waxing refers to the visible portion of the moon growing, while waning is when the moon's visible portion is shrinking.

Each phase of the moon supports particular kinds of actions—or inactions—based on the swelling or decreasing of the light. The dark of a new moon is particularly good for setting intentions, while the light of a full moon brings culmination and revelation. The days after a full moon are perfect for releasing. Calming, cleansing, and accepting are welcome attitudes in preparation for a new cycle to begin.

- New moon: the entire portion visible to Earth is covered in shadow—set intentions.

- Waxing crescent: the illuminated face is increasing, but less than half—take actions.

- Waxing gibbous: the illuminated face is increasing, and is now more than half—check in.

- Full moon: the entire portion visible to Earth is lit up—you reap what you sow.

- Waning gibbous: the illuminated face is decreasing, but still more than half—pull back.

- Waning crescent: the illuminated face is decreasing, and is now less than half—evaluate.

# SETTING A NEW MOON INTENTION

On the new moon, take space to reflect.

What do you wish to bring into your life?

Make a list of the top three goals you intend to focus your energy on over the next three weeks. Keep these goals within your personal realm of control and stay positive.

Light the candle with the match and say your goals out loud, finishing with *I ask for guidance and support in my ambitions. May they be for the greatest good of all involved.*

Blow out the candle.

Fold up the paper and tuck it under your pillow for three days.

On the fourth night, burn it over the flame of the same candle you lit on the new moon.

## MOON CAKES

The first few times you make these cakes, use them as a practice in remaining present. Bake the full moon cake two to three times before moving on to the other cakes. You may forgo the timer and the notepad once you learn the rhythm, but perhaps you will enjoy it, bringing the ritual of goal setting and journal writing with you into your baking.

This is the practice I suggest:

Pull all ingredients ahead of time and group them together.

Pull any tools you'll need and set them in place.

Read the whole recipe start to finish.

Make the Full Moon Cake first, before any other.

Incorporate all ingredients quickly and efficiently.

While it's baking, sit next to your oven with
a clock, a pen, and a notepad.

Do not open the oven door for the first twenty minutes of baking.

Make notes when the cake becomes golden brown and pulls
away slightly from the edges, when the smells of the cake
change, and to describe how it's baking in your pan.

Take the time to do some deep breathing
and reflect on your recent days.

Poke the center of the cake with a knife. When
it comes out clean, make a note of the time
and pull the cake from the oven.

# FULL MOON CAKE

Makes one 9-inch cake

He asked me what winter was like at the bakery.

"Well . . ." I paused. "I just run around starting fires."

Center a rack in the oven and preheat it to 325 degrees.

Cut a 9-inch circle of parchment to cover the bottom of the springform pan.

Grease the pan with butter, dust it with flour, and inset the parchment. Set aside.

In a medium bowl, sift together the flour, sugar, baking powder, and salt.

Add the lemon zest and set the dry ingredients aside.

Crack the eggs, putting 5 yolks in a small bowl and 9 egg whites in a separate, medium bowl.

Add the vanilla to the yolks and whisk.

Add the milk and whisk.

Add the oil and whisk.

Pour the yolk mixture into the dry ingredients and fold together till the batter is creamy, glossy, and fully combined. This will be six or seven folds with the wooden spoon, using a thoughtful and direct motion. Be sure to get the bottom and sides of the batter incorporated.

Beat the egg whites on medium/high speed with the hand blender until you see soft peaks form.

Stop.

Add the cream of tartar and resume beating till stiff peaks form.

Do not overbeat; it will dry out the egg whites.

## INGREDIENTS

**DRY**

2½ cups cake flour (page 113)

½ cup unrefined sugar

2 teaspoons baking powder

¾ teaspoon sea salt

Zest of 1 lemon

**WET**

5 egg yolks, room temperature

1 teaspoon vanilla

¾ cup whole milk, room temperature

¼ cup olive oil

**EGG WHITES**

9 egg whites, room temperature

¼ teaspoon cream of tartar

## TOOLS YOU'LL NEED

Measuring cups and spoons

Microplane grater

Parchment paper

9-inch springform pan

Room-temperature butter and flour for the pan

2 medium-size mixing bowls

Flour sifter

Small mixing bowl

Whisk

Large wooden spoon

Hand blender

Fold the stiffened whites into the batter a third at a time. The mixture should be bubbly, shiny, and loose.

Pour the batter into the prepared pan and bake the cake on the middle rack of the oven.

Use the notepad and pen and begin your practice of remaining present. Try writing about the first thing that comes to mind for 2 minutes without stopping.

Do not open the oven door for the first 20 minutes of baking.

The total baking time for the cake will be between 45 and 50 minutes. When a knife or cake tester inserted in the center comes out clean, it's done.

Within 10 minutes of taking the cake out of the oven, run a very sharp knife between the edge of the cake and the pan.

Allow the cake to cool in the pan for 1 hour or till it is cool to the touch.

Carefully remove the adjustable body of the springform pan and turn the cake over onto a cake stand or serving board.

Peel off the parchment.

Serve plain any time of day or top it with whipped cream or classic icing for an evening affair.

**TOOLS YOU'LL NEED (CONT.)**

Notepad

Pen

Thin-blade knife or cake tester

Very sharp knife

Cake stand or serving board

# NEW MOON CAKE

Makes one 9-inch cake

My bedroom stays cold on long, dark nights. Nothing makes me peel off the quilts like eating chocolate cake for breakfast.

Center a rack in the oven and preheat it to 325 degrees.

Cut a 9-inch circle of parchment to cover the bottom of the springform pan.

Grease the pan with butter, dust it with flour, and inset the parchment. Set it aside.

In a medium bowl, sift together the dry ingredients.

Crack the eggs, putting 5 yolks in a small bowl and 9 egg whites in a seperate, medium bowl.

Add the vanilla to the yolks and whisk.

Add the coffee and whisk.

Add the oil and whisk.

Pour the yolk mixture into the dry ingredients and fold together. This will be six or seven folds with the wooden spoon using a thoughtful and direct motion. Be sure to get the bottom and sides of the batter incorporated.

Pour in the cooled chocolate.

Fold again till the batter is creamy, glossy, and fully combined.

Beat the egg whites in a medium mixing bowl with the hand blender on medium/high speed until you see soft peaks.

Stop.

Add the cream of tartar and resume beating till stiff peaks form.

Do not overbeat; it will dry out the egg whites.

## INGREDIENTS

**DRY**

2½ cups cake flour (page 113)

1½ cups unrefined sugar

¼ cup unsweetened cocoa powder

2 teaspoons baking powder

¾ teaspoon salt

**WET**

5 egg yolks, room temperature

1 teaspoon vanilla

¾ cup brewed coffee, cooled

¼ cup olive oil

4 ounces 60% cacao baker's chocolate, melted and cooled (see page 123 for technique)

**EGG WHITES**

9 egg whites, room temperature

¼ teaspoon cream of tartar

## TOOLS YOU'LL NEED

Measuring cups and spoons

Parchment paper

9-inch springform pan

Room-temperature butter and flour for the pan

2 medium-size mixing bowls

Flour sifter

Small mixing bowl

Whisk

Large wooden spoon

Fold the stiffened whites into the batter a third at a time. The
mixture should be bubbly, shiny, and loose.

Pour the batter into the prepared pan and bake the cake in the
center of the oven.

Do not open the door for the first 20 minutes of baking.

The total baking time will be between 45 and 50 minutes. When a
knife or cake tester inserted in the center comes out clean, it's
done.

Within 10 minutes of taking the cake out of the oven, run a very
sharp knife between the edge of the cake and the pan.

Allow it to cool in the pan for 1 hour or till cool to the touch.

Carefully remove the adjustable body of the springform pan and turn
the cake over onto a cake stand or serving board.

Peel off the parchment.

Serve plain any time of day or top it with the ganache recipe on page 123.

**TOOLS YOU'LL NEED
(CONT.)**

Hand blender

Thin-blade knife or cake
tester

Very sharp knife

Cake stand or serving board

# WANING MOON CAKE

Makes one 9-inch cake

As the winter solstice approaches, I begin to understand worshiping the sun.

Center a rack in the oven and preheat it to 325 degrees.

Cut a 9-inch circle of parchment to cover the bottom of the springform pan.

Grease the pan with butter, dust it with flour, and insert the parchment. Set it aside.

In a medium bowl, sift together the flour, sugar, turmeric, baking powder, and salt.

Add the orange zest and set the bowl aside.

Crack the eggs, putting 5 yolks in a small bowl and 9 egg whites in a separate, medium bowl.

Add the milk and whisk.

Add the oil and whisk.

Add the honey and whisk.

Pour the yolk mixture into the dry ingredients and fold together till the batter is creamy, glossy, and fully combined. This will be six or seven folds with the wooden spoon using a thoughtful and direct motion. Be sure to get the bottom and sides of the batter incorporated.

Beat the egg whites in a medium mixing bowl with the hand blender on medium/high speed until you see soft peaks.

Stop.

Add the cream of tartar and resume beating till stiff peaks form.

Do not overbeat; it will dry out the egg whites.

Fold the stiffened whites into the batter a third at a time. The

## INGREDIENTS

**DRY**

2½ cups cake flour (page 113)

½ cup unrefined sugar

1 tablespoon turmeric

2 teaspoons baking powder

¾ teaspoon salt

Zest of 1 orange

**WET**

5 egg yolks, room temperature

¾ cup whole milk, room temperature

¼ cup olive oil

¼ cup honey

**EGG WHITES**

9 egg whites, room temperature

¼ teaspoon cream of tartar

## TOOLS YOU'LL NEED

Microplane grater

Measuring cups and spoons

Parchment paper

9-inch springform pan

Room-temperature butter and flour for the pan

2 medium-size mixing bowls

Flour sifter

Small mixing bowl

Whisk

Large wooden spoon

mixture should be bubbly, shiny, and loose.

Pour the batter into the prepared pan and bake the cake in the center of the oven.

Do not open the door for the first 20 minutes of baking.

The total baking time will be between 45 and 50 minutes. When a knife or cake tester inserted in the center comes out clean, it's done.

Within 10 minutes of taking the cake out of the oven, run a very sharp knife between the edge of the cake and the pan.

Allow to cool in the pan for 1 hour or till cool it is to the touch.

Carefully remove the adjustable body of the springform pan and turn the cake over onto a cake stand or serving board.

Peel off the parchment.

Serve plain any time of day or top with whipped cream or classic icing for an evening affair.

# WAXING MOON CAKE

Makes one 9-inch cake

In December, it seems like there is a fairy-tale mountain of wood to chop. This hearty cake keeps the axe swinging.

Center a rack in the oven and preheat it to 325 degrees.

Cut a 9-inch circle of parchment to cover the bottom of the springform pan.

Grease the pan with butter, dust it with flour, and insert the parchment. Set aside.

Chop and lightly toast the walnuts in a skillet. Set aside in a small bowl.

Combine the apple and ginger in a small bowl. Set aside.

In a medium bowl, sift together the flours, baking powder, salt, cloves, nutmeg, and cinnamon.

Crack the eggs, putting 5 yolks in a small bowl and 9 egg whites in a separate, medium bowl.

Add the milk and whisk.

Add the oil and whisk.

Add the maple syrup and whisk.

Pour the yolk mixture into the dry ingredients and fold together till the batter is creamy, glossy, and fully combined. This will be six or seven folds with the wooden spoon using a thoughtful and direct motion. Be sure to get the bottom and sides of the batter incorporated.

Beat the egg whites in a medium bowl with the hand blender on medium/high speed until you see soft peaks.

Stop.

Add the cream of tartar and resume beating till stiff peaks form.

## INGREDIENTS

### DRY

1 cup walnuts

1 Granny Smith apple

1 tablespoon ground ginger

2 cups cake flour (see page 113)

½ cup rye flour

2 teaspoons baking powder

¾ teaspoon sea salt

¼ teaspoon cloves

¼ teaspoon nutmeg

¼ teaspoon cinnamon

1 cup golden raisins

Zest of 1 lemon

### WET

5 egg yolks, room temperature

¾ cup whole milk, room temperature

¼ cup olive oil

¼ cup maple syrup

### EGG WHITES

9 egg whites, room temperature

¼ teaspoon cream of tartar

## TOOLS YOU'LL NEED

Microplane grater

Measuring cups and spoons

Parchment paper

9-inch springform pan

Room-temperature butter and flour for the pan

Do not overbeat; it will dry out the egg whites.

Fold the stiffened whites into the batter a third at a time. The mixture should be bubbly, shiny, and loose.

Fold in the apples, ginger and walnuts.

Pour the batter into the prepared pan and bake the cake in the center of the oven.

Do not open the door for the first 20 minutes of baking.

The total baking time will be between 45 and 50 minutes. When a knife or cake tester inserted in the center comes out clean, it's done.

Within 10 minutes of taking the cake out of the oven, run a very sharp knife between the edge of the cake and the pan.

Allow the cake to cool in the pan for 1 hour or till it is cool to the touch.

Carefully remove the adjustable body of the springform pan and turn the cake over onto a cake stand or serving board.

Peel off the parchment.

Serve plain any time of day.

**TOOLS YOU'LL NEED (CONT.)**

Knife

Cutting board

Skillet

3 small mixing bowls

2 medium-size mixing bowls

Flour sifter

Whisk

Large wooden spoon

Hand blender

Thin-blade knife or cake tester

Very sharp knife

Cake stand or serving board

# HUMBLE ICING

Makes enough to cover 1 single-layer 9-inch cake

I enjoy covering these cakes in the whipped cream on page 125; however, a fancy occasion requires a bit more style. The flavor of this simple icing is heavily dependent on its ingredients—use a high-quality butter and the best confectioners' sugar you can obtain. Moon cakes are intended to be stout single-layer cakes. If you wish to cut through the center and make a layer cake, you'll need to double the icing recipe.

In a large bowl, using a hand blender, cream together the butter and sugar.

Drizzle the heavy cream in a tablespoon at a time, beating after each addition. You may not need all the cream—stop adding it when the mixture reaches the texture you want.

Add the vanilla and salt; beat.

Stop creaming, set the hand blender aside, scrape down the sides of the bowl.

Resume creaming till all ingredients are fully incorporated and you have a silky icing with no lumps or dry spots.

The whole process, with the ingredients at the right temperature, should take 8 to 10 minutes.

To lighten the texture, drizzle in a little more heavy cream and quickly beat.

You can keep the icing refrigerated for up to 7 days in an airtight container.

Bring it to room temperature before using.

Apply a thin coat of icing to the entire cake using the offset spatula, starting by placing a dollop on the top, then smoothing it to the edge. Drag the icing from the top edge down over the sides of the

## INGREDIENTS

1 cup (2 sticks) unsalted butter, softened

4 cups sifted confectioners' sugar

About ¼ cup heavy cream

1 teaspoon vanilla extract

Pinch of salt

## TOOLS YOU'LL NEED

Measuring cups and spoons

Sifter

Large bowl

Hand blender

Large wooden spoon

Airtight container

Offset spatula or butter knife

Cake stand or wooden cutting board

cake. Hold the knife still and spin or turn the cake as you spread the frosting around the sides. This is called a crumb coat—it traps stray bits of cake so they don't end up in the final layer. Freeze the cake for 20 minutes.

Apply the rest of the icing, again starting with a large dollop on the top, working toward the edges, and dragging the excess down and around the sides, but spreading a thicker layer. Embellish the cake with flowers and confectioners' sugar.

## A NOTE AND ADJUSTMENTS

To make a chocolate frosting, add in 6 tablespoons dark cocoa powder. For a less sugary-sweet flavor, try adding almond or orange extract instead of vanilla. To make a more savory statement, add in a few tablespoons of fresh mint, thyme, or sage. Try frosting just the top, leaving the sides naked. Try using a stencil on top of a clean, white frosting, dusting with cinnamon to create a pattern. Or use a stencil and sprinkle confectioners' sugar on top of ganache.

## CAKE TIPS AND TROUBLESHOOTING

A fully baked cake should be relatively flat on top when done. If your cake is doming or falling in, consider a few things:

**The flour.**
You may be using flour that is too high in protein. The web of gluten formed when high-protein flour and water are combined prevents the leavening gases from escaping. Flour with a lower protein content has a weaker gluten structure, allowing the gas to leave easily without tearing or causing swells. Be sure to use a cake flour, whether you make your own from page 113 or purchase it at the grocery.

**The pan.**
A pan that conducts heat unevenly will bake the sides faster than the middle, causing the cake to volcano in the center. Look for a sturdier pan that can hold the heat evenly.

**The leavening.**
Make sure your chemical leavening is up to date and/or that your egg whites were whipped to stiff peaks perfectly.

**The heat source.**
A chiffon cake like this one is the blend of a batter-style and sponge-style cake: leavened by the air from the whipped egg whites alongside the chemical effects of baking powder. If you bake it at too high a heat, you'll have a compact cake with a thick crust and cracked top. If your oven is too cool, your cake is likely to fall and have a coarse, dry crumb.

For best results, go slow and low while baking. It's a low temp for a prolonged period of time that allows the color and flavors to properly marry. Make sure you are baking your cake on the center rack in the middle of the oven so heat can circulate evenly.

We can all agree on some aspects that make a cake great. It should look like its intended shape with no mountain peaks or hidden holers. The crust should be entirely golden brown, thin, and a little crispy. The crumb of the cake should be incredibly moist, light, and uniform. With high-quality eggs, it should even taste a little "eggy." When pressed upon gently, the cake should slowly spring back. To experience the full flavor of a cake, let it cool for at least three hours before tasting it.

## SMOKE SIGNALS CORE VALUES

Are you breathing?

Think of flour as fresh produce.

Learn one recipe like the back of your hand.

Art and science are meant to reinforce each other,
   not undermine each other. All binaries are false.

Keep a journal and be observant.

Work is the only truth. Learn to trust.

Engage the intelligence of your body.

Value the entire process, not just the final result.

Strive, but take breaks.

Keep a clear mind and a clean work space.

Lived experience informs technique.

Strength through diversity, not
   monoculture; be a little wild.

The end is just the beginning.

# INDEX

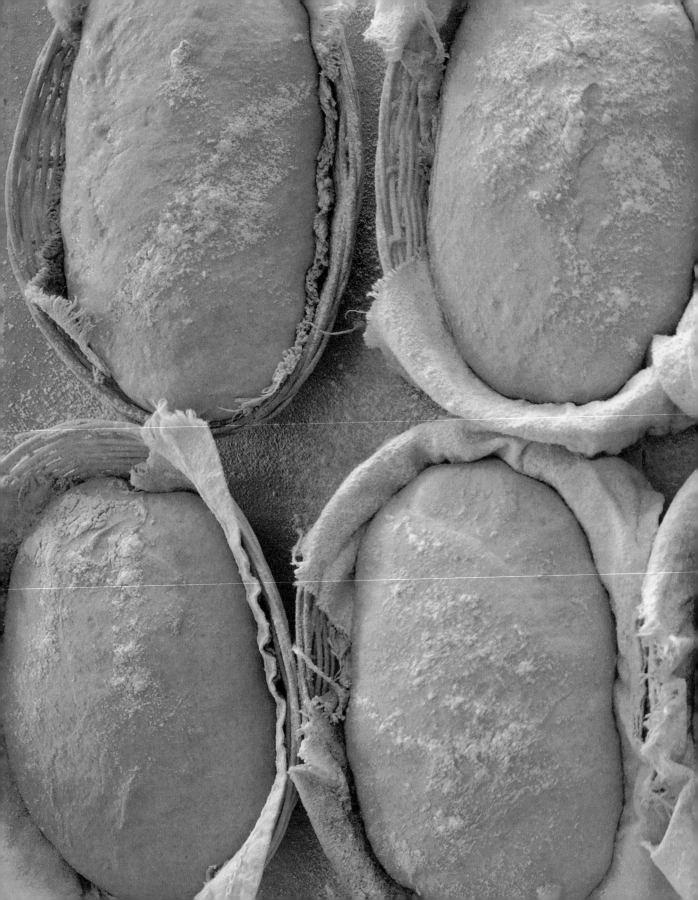